THE STUDENT TEACHER ON THE FIRING LINE

By D. Eugene Meyer

D. Eugene Meyer
Professor of Education
Department of Curriculum and Instruction
Northern Illinois University
DeKalb, Illinois   60115

CENTURY TWENTY ONE PUBLISHING

PUBLISHED BY

CENTURY TWENTY ONE PUBLISHING
POST OFFICE BOX 8
SARATOGA, CALIFORNIA 95070

LIBRARY OF CONGRESS CARD CATALOG NUMBER

80-69236

I.S.B.N.

0-86548-048-6

TABLE OF CONTENTS

THE STUDENT TEACHER ON THE FIRING LINE

PREFACE

This book is designed to help the student teacher gain a student teaching experience of high quality. It provides you with an orientation to your student teaching position; it helps in defining your responsibilities and assists you in carrying them out properly.

The handbook is divided into five parts, each with a specific purpose.

Part I.   INTRODUCTION AND OVERVIEW - Contains general suggestions and tips for effective student teaching. This part should be read very carefully. The content can then be discussed in the orientation and seminar sessions before you enter the schools for your student teaching experience. As you read through it, write down in the margins any questions you might have. You will have an opportunity to obtain answers to these questions from your university supervisor, the principal, and/or your cooperating teacher. You may profit from reviewing this part after the beginning of student teaching.

Part II.   ORIENTATION TO THE SCHOOL - Contains a series of check lists and questions which are designed to ensure your obtaining an initial familiarity with the important features of the school in which you are student teaching. The objectives called for are to be completed during the first phase of the student teaching period.

Part III.   POLICIES, PROCEDURES, AND REQUIREMENTS - Contains important information on specific aspects of student teaching. Each of the topics introduced in this portion will be discussed during the pre-student teaching orientation.

You may find it necessary to refer to specific items in the book from time to time throughout the student teaching period.

Part IV.   FORMS AND RECORDS - Contains a description of the forms that are used by the student teacher in carrying out a variety of responsibilities and duties. The university will furnish individualized blank forms for use by the student teacher, the cooperating teacher, and the university supervisor.

Part V.   MAJOR PROBLEMS IN TEACHING - Contains an overview of the teaching profession, public relations, and teacher evaluation. Information in this section is designed to help you develop your working philosophy of education as well as evaluate the philosophy of the school. Psychology of learning as well as child growth and development will be presented along with a section presenting ways to keep up with new methods and techniques. While in the schools you will be able to refer to these to discuss the skills and techniques of teaching as well as the suggestions for becoming a self-renewing teacher.

The author expresses his appreciation to the California Teachers Association, and the Office of the Career Planning and Placement Center, Northern Illinois University for permission to use materials for this book.

CHAPTER 1

INTRODUCTION AND OVERVIEW

Front and Center

You are "On Stage." The spotlight is on you. This is it! You are not "Just another student." In the eyes of the elementary, junior high, or senior high students with whom you will be working, their parents, and the community, you are a TEACHER! Your student teaching experience can and should be among the most important and rewarding of your teacher education program. But, what you get out of it will be largely up to you - your willingness to work, your eagerness to learn, and your humanistic approach to teaching. Congratulations and good luck!

Why Student Teaching?

As one of the culminating phases of your professional preparation for teaching, your student teaching activity provides opportunities to try your wings. Here you will be able to make an easy transition from the "mind set" of a student to the status of a conscientious and capable teacher. You will cross the magic line between student and teacher. This is not to say that you will no longer be a student. The outstanding teacher is forever learning, improving, and growing professionally. You will have a chance to apply some of the theories and principles learned in the classroom. You will have a chance to see how effectively you can perform in front of a group of boys and girls who can be eager and questioning, or skeptical and irritating. How well

1

you can adapt to these various moods and conditions will, in a sense, determine

your qualifications for the profession. Some of you may have had previous

teaching experience at the sophomore and junior level doing observation work

with an individual and/or small group. This should help you in settling into

your student teaching job. Senior students should think in terms of observa-

tion, bit teaching, working with individuals, working with small groups,

working with the total group, and attending all school functions. The student

teacher should study carefully the teacher's plan and be willing to follow it

since the teacher is legally in charge of the classroom. At the same time you

will utilize your background of training in education to develop the units

planned as well as handling the every day routine procedures. Here is your

opportunity to try out new ideas, to test, to experiment, although you must

confer and work closely with your cooperating teacher and your university

supervisor. This is a time in your career that you should gather all types

of information and ideas for your files, and you should manage to visit other

teachers in the school for methods, ideas, and techniques. You should also

plan to visit other schools which have different philosophies and building

designs.

Some Obligations...

...To your university. As you go about your student teaching duties,

you will be acting, in no small way, as a representative of your university.

Your conduct as a student teacher should develop good will and confidence

toward the university. You are a guest of the cooperating school. Your atti-

tude and actions should continually promote desirable public relations between that school and the university.

...To the cooperating school. The primary purpose of the school in which you have been invited to teach is to develop learning activities for boys and girls. It is your responsibility to work with your cooperating teacher, your university supervisor, the administration, and the community for the best interest of the children of that school. Know the school regulations and policies. Be prompt and regular in attendance. Be sure that your plans are available for the cooperating teacher. Be enthusiastic, take initiative, be willing to speak up, and accept responsibilities. Plan carefully for group teaching and have your plans checked and approved by your cooperating teacher.

...To the students. The first few days will be spent in getting acquainted, observing the activities of your cooperating teacher, and learning the names of your students. Acquaint yourself with their individual personalities and problems. Be sure you are aware of proper, approved disciplinary techniques and classroom management. Be professional; never discuss confidential information with those who have no need for it or who might use it improperly.

...To yourself. Your campus and social activities should not interfere with your student teaching work. If problems arise concerning your student teaching, contact your university supervisor or your cooperating teacher. Save times for meetings and conferences with your supervisors. Look and act like the teacher. "Joe College" dress may be all right for campus dress, but it is not all right for the student teacher. Neatness and cleanliness are very important. See what other teachers are wearing and how they are groomed. Keep in excellent physical and mental health at all times. Be alert and

3

energetic; do the job well. Be dignified, but have a friendly attitude.

The First Days on the Job!!!

You can bet the first days on the job are important. You may be eager to get started; but don't rush in half ready and unprepared. Give yourself a chance to become adjusted to your new surroundings and do the work expected of you. You should not expect to walk into the classroom and within a few days take over. Rather, there should be a gradual introduction to teaching. A deliberately arranged series of orientation activities are included in Part II of this book.

The first morning on the job you should report to the secretary and principal. The principal will have planned some type of orientation program for you and will direct you to those with whom you will be working. Your first days provide important opportunities to get acquainted - with your co-workers, the school plant, the daily routines, emergency measures, the students, and the community.

You may approach your student teaching experience with uncertainty, hesitancy, possibly even with fear. Your cooperating teacher and university supervisor will do everything they can to make you feel at ease and part of the teaching profession. They will carefully observe your orientation and your progress. When it is believed that you are "ready," the opportunity to teach under the guidance of the cooperating teacher will be given to you. Be ready to listen to suggestions made for your improvement. Continuous self-evaluation is important too. Remember, assumption of teaching responsibilities should be gradual. Additional responsibilities will be given to you as you diligently demonstrate your interest, ability, and readiness to assume them. There will be additional opportunities provided to observe the cooperating teacher after you have done some teaching. This will give you a chance to look for answers to specific questions or for particular things that you will have in mind.

How Can I Be Sure of Success?

We can never be sure of it. Success can be rather illusive at times, but there are certain factors that can help to make successes in your student teaching work. Read on!

Planning your work. Good teaching, as in good work of any kind, is based upon careful planning. Lesson plans are essential to give direction and organization to your work and to provide for maximum student growth. Your daily plans must be in terms of major topics, units, or course outlines used by or approved by your cooperating teacher. However, your cooperating teacher may wish to have you use a different lesson plan than the one you developed in your classroom at the university. The exact outline details can be worked out between the two of you. Basically lesson plan guidelines are about the same.

Lesson plans should be handed to the cooperating teacher at least two days in advance. Some cooperating teachers in the schools will request that all plans be prepared one week in advance or longer. The cooperating teacher will usually check the plans and will initial them, indicating approval or necessary changes. Changes can be discussed and arranged before the lesson is taught, and follow-up discussions can be more meaningful. Be sure that your plans are complete and hand them in far enough in advance to be thoroughly checked by the cooperating teacher.

Conferences can help. Plan time for conferences with your cooperating teacher and with your university supervisor, and report for them promptly. Feel free to request a conference at any time you feel a particular need to do so. The cooperating teacher will hold many informal and brief conferences in the early stages of your orientation and beginning teacher activities. Things such as general classroom procedure, classroom management, lesson planning, and evaluation can be discussed. Carry out faithfully any suggestions given by the cooperating teacher or by the university supervisor.

Any listing of suggestions is incomplete. You will need to be continually alert to develop additional "successful ideas" which can be most appropriate for you, but here are some hints:

1. Be well prepared.

2. Beware of the overused lecture method. Many other good teaching techniques and methods have been developed.

3. Be "fair, firm, and friendly."

4. Enjoy your work: smile; laugh.

5. Avoid being too personal with students. Remember the "desk" line.

6. Don't try to talk above a noisy classroom.

7. Be consistant.

8. Be helpful; be understanding.

9. Stress the positive.

10. Recognize the interest span of the group you are working with.

11. Admit your mistakes. (A wise man will admit his mistakes; a fool

never does.)

12. Avoid sarcasm.

13. Avoid group punishment for the misbehavior of one (or a few).

14. Call upon a student whose attention is wavering.

15. Move about while teaching. Most good teachers can do a better job when they are on their feet!

16. Vary the tone and volume of your voice.

17. Be genuinely interested in your work; be enthusiastic. The students will be encouraged to follow your example.

18. Avoid tobacco breath, cheap perfume, and other undesirable odors of body and breath.

19. Be well-groomed; avoid overuse of make-up.

20. Make your classroom, and your appearance, attractive and interesting.

21. Use your eyes and ears to keep informed of the situation. Let all about you know that you are confident and are the master of the situation.

22. Talk to your class, not over their heads; yet consistently challenge their best efforts.

23. Be flexible.

24. Individualize.

25. Let everyone know you are proud to be a teacher.

Evaluation of Your Work

Regular evaluation is a prerequisite for improvement of any because it enables you to know how well you are doing and how you can do better. It is essential that you analyze your performance critically. You must see the need for growth; you must have a desire to improve. Your cooperating teacher and your university supervisor will assist you in pinpointing weaknesses and strengths. Conferences with these persons will raise questions and provide suggestions for improving specific aspects of your teaching. You should make daily self evaluations of your lesson plans and your classroom performance. Thus, as you recognize weaknesses, you can quickly make a conscious effort to overcome them.

There is a rating scale on which mid-term and final evaluations will be made. This form should be shown to you and discussed with you before your student teaching. (See Part IV, Student Teacher Evaluation Forms) Frequent reference to its items will be made during formal and informal conferences concerning your progress. You will be asked to use it to rate yourself. Remember, knowing what to do is not enough; neither is achievement always in direct proportion to effort. However, the knowledge of what to do and of how to go about it, together with nothing less than your best efforts, will help obtain great achievement in the classroom.

Both you and the cooperating teacher need to be aware that you are a student teacher, and that progress, rather than initial excellence, is the important thing. Do not be disappointed if you or your cooperating teacher checks many areas for attention and needed improvement. If you were a master teacher now, there would be little reason for you to do student teaching.

You will be evaluated in terms of what should be expected of you as a student teacher and in terms of your potential as a teacher. It may be impossible to devise any evaluation instrument that will adequately measure the progress and potential of all students. Nevertheless, it is important that the student teacher, the cooperating teacher, and the college supervisor have some specific guides and standards. The rating should serve as a guide for improvement and as a basis for frank and open discussions about the progress you are making.

Some Clarification of the Rating Scale

The following brief comments about the major section of the rating scale may help you to focus your efforts toward high standards in these important areas of professional characteristics:

Teaching Techniques. Here an attempt is made to suggest specific techniques, skills, and methods that can contribute to the improvement of learning activities. Points listed here should be specific help to you in your daily planning and class activities.

Scholarship. One must possess knowledge of the subject if he expects to direct learning activities related thereto. The teacher must also be able to communicate effectively with his students. Being able to speak intelligently on many topics with parents and other community citizens can enhance your chances for professional and personal success.

Classroom Management. The teacher must be aware of the class climate and the class morale. The teacher's responsibility for pupil behavior must be realized and accepted. You should become familiar with effective techniques employed by others.

Personal Qualities. The appearance of the teacher in the classroom is very important. Children are inclined to emulate the teacher. Be a model for them. Be sure your behavior patterns are accepted in terms of professional conduct and the community codes. "A teacher affects eternity; he can never tell where his influence stops." - Henry Adams.

Professional Relationships. As a student teacher you must give consideration to those attitudes and habits accepted as standard in the profession. Become familiar with and participate in the allied activity programs of the school. It is hoped that you will become a full-fledged member of the profession. Always act according to the Code of Ethics.

CHAPTER 2

ORIENTATION TO THE SCHOOL

What to Look For

The student teacher must be introduced to all activities of the school in order to obtain a good foundation for his profession of teaching. As soon as possible after his arrival, the student teacher should be given faculty and student handbooks so he can familiarize himself with the school policies, regulations, and privileges as a teacher. A tour of the school plant is also in order. This tour should include the location of all offices, introduction to all staff, and especially the special services that are available for children.

The learning center and use of media equipment is most important. The student teacher will want to familiarize himself with the policies and procedures of the learning center as well as the types of equipment and material that are available. He then can use the various media to enrich and to supplement his teaching. Of special importance is the procedure for requisition of supplies and equipment and for arrangement of field trips which will enrich the teaching experience.

It is well that the student teacher keep a calendar of events which would contain information on specific professional pursuits and assignments of teaching activities. This way any questions can be jotted down in the margin and discussed with the cooperating teacher and/or the university supervisor.

In order to have a systematic, organized orientation of facilities the

11

student teacher can use the following check list upon entering the student teaching assignment. The student's response can be recorded and then referred to or discussed with the cooperating teacher and the university supervisor.

Philosophy of School

The primary aim of education in the broadest sense of this word is to "form a man" or rather to help a child of man attain his full formation of his completeness as a man. The other aims (to convey the heritage of culture of a given area of civilization, to prepare for life in society and for good citizenship, and secure mental equipment required for implementing a particular function in the social life) are corollaries and essential but secondary aims. Parenthetically, it must be observed that education in the broad sense of the word continues during the entire lifetime of every one of us. The School System deals essentially with that which can be taught, it refers to the education and formation of intelligence more than of the will.

It is clear that the primary aim is determined by human nature. The question, "what is man?" is the unavoidable preamble to any philosophy of education. The teacher exercises a real causal power on the mind of the pupil, but in the manner in which a doctor acts to heal his patient: by assisting nature and cooperating with it. Education like medicine, is ars co-operativa natural.

The contention of Thomist philosophy is that they (the vital energies of nature in the patient, the intellectual energies of nature in the pupil) are the principal agents, on whose own activity the process primarily depends. The principal agent in the educational process is not the teacher, but the

12

student. Progressive education has had the distinction of putting the forgotten truth in question into the foreground. The "Principal agent" is not able to give himself what he does not have. He would lead himself astray if he acted at random. He must be taught and guided. But the main thing in this teaching process is that his natural and spontaneous activity be always respected and his power of insight and judgement always fostered, so that at each step he may master the subject matter in which he is instructed. In this perspective, what matters most is to develop in the child the "intuitivity" of the mind and its spiritual discriminating and creative energies. The educational venture is a ceaseless appeal to intelligence and free will in the young person.

Orientation Check List

1. Physical Facilities. Check these items and answer the following questions:

    1. For what school function is each school building and each portion of the building used?

    2. Where is each of the following?

        Superintendent's Office_____
        Principal's Office_____
        Guidance Office_____
        Study Halls_____
        Library(ies) and/or Learning Centers_____
        Media Center_____
        Health Facilities_____
        Lunch Room_____

    3. Find and read the fire drill and disaster drill regulations. What are "your" students supposed to do in case of a fire alarm?_____
        _____

13

4. Who is the building custodian? _____

   Where is his work room? _____

2. Classroom Management. Check these items and answer these questions:

   1. What evidence of the standard of pupil behavior do you observe?

   2. How are student behavior problems handled?

   3. Under what arrangements may individual students leave the room during the on-going sessions?

   4. Under what arrangements do students pass from the classroom(s) to other areas of the school?

   5. Under what arrangements are students allowed to communicate during class sessions?

3. Classroom Organizations. Check these items and answer these questions:

   1. What rules and policies govern the seating arrangement of students?

   2. Prepare a seating chart of the class, even the groups which you are not directly working with.

   3. Learn the names of each student in each group.

   4. How does the cooperating teacher keep attendance records?

   5. How does the cooperating teacher keep a record of makeup work assigned and completed?

   6. How does the cooperating teacher keep a progress report or records of grades or marks?

   7. Where are ventilation and temperature controls located in your classrooms and how are they operated?

   8. What facilities such as bulletin boards, display tables, and so forth, are available for use in the classrooms you will use?

4. Information about students. Check these items and answer these questions:

1. Is a cummulative record kept on each student?

2. Where are these records stored?

3. List the kinds of data kept on each student and describe the use of each kind.

<u>Kind of Data</u>   <u>Use of Data</u>

5. Policies and regulations. Check each of these items and answer these questions:

   1. Obtain a copy of the faculty handbook. Check it through to see what it contains.

   2. What hours are teachers expected to be in school?

   3. What policies govern attendance, absence, and sickness?

   4. What limitations and recommendations are made on assigning homework?

   5. What restrictions and provisions are made for conducting field trips?

   6. What limitations and recommendations are made for punishment and discipline?

   7. What is the recommended procedure in case of an accident?

   8. What safety precautions are recommended concerning the classroom areas in which you will teach?

   9. What is the policy concerning students entering the building at morning and at noon time?

6. Student handbook

   11. Obtain a copy of the student handbook. Examine its contents carefully.

       (This section applies only to those schools having student handbooks; generally only the upper elementary grades will be involved. If there is no handbook applicable to the grade level you are teaching, indicate such by writing "NONE" across the face of this section.)

For what areas of student activities are there rules and regulations in the handbook? _____ _____
_____ _____ _____ _____
_____ _____ _____ _____

What activities and organizations are described in the student handbook?_____
_____
_____

What school services are described in the student handbook?
_____ _____
_____ _____

What honors and awards are described and listed in the handbook?
_____ _____
_____ _____

Check which of the following are contained in the student handbook?

Daily schedule_____   School Songs_____
Report card info_____   Pep cheers_____
Faculty_____   Grading system_____
Required curriculum_____   School philosophy_____
Elective curriculum_____   Graduation requirements_____
Calendar of events_____   Student fees_____

Instructional Activities: While making three different classroom observations

of your own selection, complete one of these sheets for each observation.

FIRST CLASSROOM OBSERVATION

What action does the teacher take to get the lesson underway?
_____
_____

How does the teacher begin the learning activities of the lesson?
_____
_____
_____

How long does it take the teacher to get all or most of the students involved in the lesson?_____

_____

_____

Does the teacher ask questions?_____What are the characteristics of the questioning process?_____

_____

_____

What instructional materials are used to teach the lesson?_____

_____

_____

After twenty minutes of the lesson has passed, what portion of the students are actually engaged in the learning process?_____

_____

What techniques does the teacher use to stimulate learning?_____

_____

_____

What provisions does the teacher make for individual differences?

_____

What evidence of student-teacher planning do you detect?_____

_____

What variety of learning experiences is used in teaching the lesson?

_____

What types of evaluation does the teacher use?_____

_____

_____

SECOND CLASSROOM OBSERVATION

What action does the teacher take to get the lesson under way?_____

_____

_____

How does the teacher begin the learning activities of the lesson?

_____

_____

How long does it take the teacher to get all or most of the students involved in the lesson?_____

17

Does the teacher ask questions?_____What are the characteristics
of the questioning process?_____

_____

_____

What instructional materials are used to teach the lesson?_____

_____

After twenty minutes of the lesson has passed, what proportion of
the students are actually engaged in the learning process?_____

_____

What techniques does the teacher use to stimulate learning?_____

_____

What provisions does the teacher make for individual differences?

_____

What evidence of student-teacher planning do you detect?_____

_____

What variety of learning experiences is used in teaching the lesson?

_____

What types of evaluation does the teacher use?_____

_____

_____

THIRD CLASSROOM OBSERVATION

What action does the teacher take to get the lesson under way?_____

_____

_____

How does the teacher begin the learning activities of the lesson?

_____

_____

How long does it take the teacher to get all or most of the students
involved in the lesson?_____
Does the teacher ask questions?_____What are the characteristics
of the questioning process?_____

_____

What instructional materials are used to teach the lesson?_____

_____

After twenty minutes of the lesson has passed, what proportion
of the students are actually engaged in the learning process?

_____

What techniques does the teacher use to stimulate learning?_____

_____

What provisions does the teacher make for individual differences?

_____

What evidence of student-teacher planning do you detect?_____

_____

What variety of learning experiences are used in teaching the lesson?

_____

_____

What type of evaluation does the teacher use?_____

_____

_____

The Instructional Program

An Instructional Program is an aggregate of components and sub-components,
with interactions, for the purpose of facilitating some specified behavior
change in the learner. When designing an instructional sequence, which learner
characteristic should be considered? Reading level is often considered relevant and important. What about sex, age, interest, social class, background,
cognitive style and numerous other factors? What about teacher characteristics
and/or teaching styles. Only research ultimately can provide answers to these
questions. One research project has isolated 260 variables and all their possible combinations which were considered most relevant factors in making instructional decisions.

Instructional Programs are written with specific systems in mind. The
objectives are carefully stated, and the progression through learning tasks

19

is carefully designed to assure successful completions of 90% or more of the "frames" by 90% of the individuals using the program. Certainly not all programmed instruction materials are perfect or even adequate. In essence, we may rely on two kinds of technology. After the teacher analyzes the individual instructional system, he then 1) creates a new set of procedures, materials, etc., to accomplish the desired objectives or 2) he adapts an existing technology such as a programmed text which will best fit the system.

Learners verification is an essential part of any learning experience. Teachers need to keep themselves apprised of student progress so that they can mold future learning experiences to be most meaningful in meeting individual student need. Evaluation of students also helps the teacher learn where he or she has been ineffective in motivating the student to learn effectively and provides keys for revising previous materials and teaching techniques to enable the teacher to do a better job. Positive feedback on learning achievements can be of immeasurable help in motivating students toward continued and stronger effort.

Activities may be followed by testing. The degree to which the objectives of instructional programming have been met can be judged by observing the quality of participation of students in discussions, projects, dramatization and other activity oriented learning applications.

Participation

Please write in the date for each of the following:

Check workbooks_____ Write assignments on board_____
Mark papers_____ Regulate ventilation_____
Score tests_____ Dismiss the class_____
Record marks in record Duplicate worksheets_____
  book_____ Take charge of small group_____
Supervise the playground___ Prepare for a program_____
Supervise the lunchroom___ Make charts and posters_____
Supervise the hallway_____ Supervise cleaning up_____
Distribute materials_____ Get materials ready_____
Distribute books_____ Check class attendance_____
Arrange bulletin boards____ Contribute enrichment materials_____

Assisting the Students:

Find and make available reference materials for students_____
Explain and demonstrate proper use of equipment_____
Help individual students with seatwork and study habits_____
Provide guidance for students conducting research_____
Accompany groups on field trips_____
Work with small groups on projects_____

Attending School Functions:

Faculty meeting_____ Athletic event_____
Parent-Teacher conference_____ Pep meeting_____
PTA meeting_____ Class meeting_____
Assembly or program_____ Contest, fair, festival_____
School party_____ Education association, meeting_____
Club, interest group meeting_____
Institute days_____

Getting Ready

Course Plans (For each of the classes that you will be teaching.) Look

through the textbooks and locate the present and future portions for study.

Study _____
Look through the manual, workbooks, study guide, etc. _____
Review the State or City course of study pertaining to
  your classes _____
Go over the long range plans with cooperating teacher _____
Locate the equipment that will be used _____
Obtain outside references for the portion you will be
  teaching _____
Develop a unit plan with the assistance of your supervising
  teacher _____

Read to review and supplement your background in the subject _____

Develop some of the first individual lesson plans with the assistance of your supervising teacher _____

Schedule: Record in the spaces below the regularly scheduled occurences in the school day, and the time of each. _____

_____
_____
_____
_____
_____
_____
_____
_____
_____
_____
_____

Using Supportive Services

There are numerous services available outside the classroom, to help your student teaching experiences be successful. Within the school building itself, the Library, Learning Center or Media Center can provide invaluable assistance. Many of these have a large selection of instructional materials available. If not, every school has access to film and material catalogues which can provide teaching aids from outside the school. Assistance from many state and local agencies is available through the school nurse or school psychologist. These agencies can provide instructional and resource aids to help achieve objectives and assist in meeting the needs of the children.

Most universities provide several services for student teachers. Through these services student teachers can usually check out instructional aids for a specified length of time. Media Centers provide all types of teaching media for use by student teachers.

Teacher Education Programs have several laboratories and clinics where materials and assistance are available to students. Utilizing these services can enhance your teaching experiences and provide new experiences for the students you are working with. They usually include:

1. Materials Laboratory

2. Metric Education Laboratory

3. Science Education Laboratory

4. Materials Production Laboratory

5. Media Center

6. Test Laboratory

7. Film Library

8. Exercise Laboratory

9. Computorized Learning Laboratory

10. Learning Center

As a student teacher you should choose carefully the materials and ideas acquired through supportive services. Close evaluation of the plans you bring into the classroom can help ensure that they best suit the needs of the students and stay within the guide lines of the curriculum.

Communication, The Vital Link

More elements of communication problems within a school district center around building than any other place in a school's organization. The persons who occupy teaching and administrative positions at the building level have greater contact with more students, more staff and more sponsors. As a result they are the basic determiners of a school's impact on community. It is this proximity to every communication avenue that suggests that a major skill of building level personnel must lie in the many areas of communication and human relations.

In examining communication skills, a first concern should be a person's listening skills. Have you listened lately to the messages from the young? Hearing messages from the young does not mean agreement. It does, however, mean listening with understanding. One message is "see me." It is "see me" as a person. The child who demands attention is giving a "see me" message. Most of us have outgrown our need to be seen - or have we? Perhaps we have just solved our personal problem - and others need to solve theirs. And we need to help. The "see me" message demands a response. The problem, then, becomes one of responding to the attention needs of children in ways that are agreeable to you, rather than in terms that are detrimental to both the teacher and the student. The messages value should be taken as an important thing by teachers and parents. There are many more messages from our students, and we - as school leaders must become adept to listening to them and responding to them in ways that are productive for all of us.

The most important listening skill for the school administrator is rec-ognizing one basic principle. A problem is a problem when someone states it. Your response to a problem does not have to please, and it does not have to be a violation of your own integrity; but your arguments, your persuasions and your actions must reflect real knowledge and empathy for the frame of reference in which a problem is presented.

If only we could communicate with each other, it seems that many of our problems would simply disappear. We will have better lives at home, in school, and in communities. The generation gap would disappear, we hope, if kids once again started communicating with their parents. The schools could be places of joy, not of violence and confrontation. If we were communicating with each other and were together again we could make progress toward getting rid of problems of drug abuse, juvenile crime and sexual promiscuity. If only we lived with communication, we could again have communities with people living as good neighbors and not under a perpetual state of siege.

The world view of an individual, communicators now know, is typically determined by such factors as age, education, occupation, socioeconomic status of himself and his parents, religion, language, political orientation, and his cultural background. Even within the same language system we use the language with different facility and with different accents. Words are often labels for concepts. The more words one knows, the more generalizations or discriminations one might be able to handle. If the other person does not know all the words you know, you may be able to communicate with him only about a few things, again only in broad terms.

The school administrators and staff should not only learn to communicate effectively but should examine their perceptions. The teachers and parents need to communicate with children from a new stance of equality, mutuality and shared responsibility. A teacher has to realize that the student is not the docile, obedient, inexperienced kid of years past. He is grown-up. He is living in a communication - saturated society.

CHAPTER 3

POLICIES, PROCEDURES, AND REQUIREMENTS

Assignment for Student Teaching

Each student is assigned to a cooperating teacher in his major area in a cooperating school for a period of nine, twelve, or eighteen weeks; the student teacher's duties are decided in general by agreement among the cooperating school administrator, the student teacher, and the university supervisor. Usually the student teacher's load will be the same as the teaching load of the cooperating teacher. In order to obtain appropriate student teaching experience in, for instance a student teacher's minor area, the person may be assigned to some other experience under another cooperating teacher or an assistant cooperating teacher.

The student teaching assignment should provide a wide variety of desirable learning experiences. In addition to the regular instructional duties, the student teacher will be guided by the cooperating teacher into engaging in an appropriate variety of extra-class and other activities of the school and community.

The student teacher has the same responsibilities for attendance and punctuality as a regularly employed teacher. The student teacher is expected to be on time for all scheduled obligations. As is true for regular teaching, circumstances may arise which prevent student teacher's perfect attendance and punctuality. Should such occur, the student teacher has the same obligation

26

as a regularly employed teacher.

In order to be considered as justification for non-attendance, an illness must be incapacitating or, in the opinion of a medical doctor, seriously contagious. "Feeling punk" is not a justifiable reason for absence.

Extenuating circumstances of an emergency nature, such as a mechanical breakdown, an accident, or blocked roads, may delay or prevent the attendance of the student teacher. In such circumstances, as in cases of incapacitating illness, the student teacher is obligated to notify the administrator or cooperating school immediately or if possible well in advance of his scheduled appearance in school. Failure to notify properly will be judged as negligence of responsibility.

Conflicting obligations may prevent the student teacher's attendance. Such obligations as the funeral of a close relative, or appearance in court, or a medical appointment may be considered justifiable cause for non-attendance; meeting an appointment with a hairdresser, a barber, or a dentist, would not be cause for such obligations can be rescheduled.

Absences due to conflicting obligations may be anticipated in advance of the absence, and for these the student teacher is expected to obtain permission from the proper officials by completing and obtaining signatures on the form for absence from student teaching. For such an absence the student teacher is expected to plan in advance for the cooperating teacher to teach the appropriately sequential lessons. During the spring semester, especially student teachers may need to schedule job interviews. It is important to note that if these are scheduled well in advance and if the cooperating teacher and university supervisor are adequately informed, the student teacher will usually be excused.

Student Teacher Code of Ethics*

Student Teacher and Student

1. All information about students is to be kept confidential.

2. Be more concerned with what is being achieved with the students than what impression is being made on the cooperating teacher or the university supervisor.

3. Maintain the dignity necessary to gain the respect of students; always act like an adult.

4. Show high regard for each student; show enthusiasm for each area of the curriculum you teach.

5. Be sympathetic and courteous toward all students.

6. Consider yourself a member of the community of which you are teaching and act accordingly.

7. Disciplinary measures and classroom management used by the student teacher should conform to the policies and instructions of the cooperating teacher.

8. Be a good example to your students in every way, physically, mentally, ethically.

9. Be just as interested in and just as ready to assist with the improvement of the class as if it were your own.

10. Recognize that each child is an individual and take into consideration individual abilities, interests, and capacity for learning.

11. Be impartial in disciplinary action when dealing with students and strive to be fair when judging a student's action.

12. Refrain from imposing your own religious or political views upon students; exhibit a broad-minded, tolerant attitude toward other groups and individuals.

Student Teacher and University Supervisor

1. Consider the university supervisor as one who is helping you to become a competent teacher.

2. Attention of the students must not be drawn to the university supervisor, or to a visiting parent, unless instructions are received to the contrary.

3. Provide the university supervisor with plans, textbooks, or materials being used. This should be done before the class starts. There should not be reason to converse with the university supervisor during class.

4. When the class begins, concentrate on the lesson and disregard the fact that you are being observed by the university supervisor.

5. Provide time when you and the university supervisor may have a conference in order to discuss the problems of teaching.

6. Be appreciative of criticism and seek suggestions.

Student Teacher and Cooperating Teacher

1. Remember that the cooperating teacher is in legal control of the class and is legally responsible for it.

2. You and the cooperating teacher should respect one another's professional rights and personal dignity.

3. Accept the cooperating teacher's decisions concerning the material

to be covered and the method of presentation.

4. Assume no authority that has not been specifically delegated by the cooperating teacher.

5. Know definitely what is expected of you by the cooperating teacher.

6. Complete cooperation should be established between you and the cooperating teacher; conferences should include informal talks as well as scheduled formal ones.

7. The cooperating teacher is eager to help; suggestions and criticism should be accepted by you with this in mind.

8. Support the cooperating teacher in matters of school discipline.

9. Have your lesson plans checked by the cooperating teacher in conducting the class. Be imaginative and creative in making suggestions and planning.

10. Give due credit to the cooperating teacher for all assistance given to you.

11. If you feel you are having difficulty in the situation, you should first consult your cooperating teacher. If the results are not satisfactory, you should talk immediately with your university supervisor.

Personal Attributes and Professional Growth

1. Respect those with whom you work - cooperating teacher, supervisors, administrators, and fellow student teachers.

2. Remember that student teaching is a learning situation; be willing and eager to receive suggestions and carry them out.

3. Adapt your behavior and practices to the situation in which you do your student teaching. Be guided by what is considered acceptable in your

particular room, school, and district.

4. Be an active member of a recognized local, state, or national, educational organization.

5. Acquaint yourself with a professional literature in education and in special fields.

6. Manifest general pride in the teaching profession. Consider yourself a member of the profession and act in all matters in accordance with its code of ethics.

7. Know the legal responsibilities of teachers in your state.

8. Strive always to broaden your knowledge and be well informed on current events.

9. Attend and participate in non-classroom school duties of the cooperating teacher.

10. Be well groomed and practice sound principles of hygiene, mental health, and moral integrity.

11. Display a democratic attitude toward all the teachers in the school in which you are placed.

*Handbook for chapter officers and committee chairman, student teachers' association California Teachers Association, San Francisco, 1950.

Participation in University Activities - During the period of student teaching, the student is expected to devote his full attention to the student teaching assignment, to participate fully in the school and community activities where he is student teaching. The complete benefits of a student teaching experience cannot be obtained if part of the attention of the student teacher is diverted

to continued participation in the extra-class activities of the university.
Therefore, the student teacher is expected to discontinue participation in all
university activities during the periods of student teaching. Exceptions may
be made for certain students whose continued participation in a specific
activity is necessary for the effective continuation of that activity on the
campus. Permission to participate in university activity (one that would
require their absence from the classroom) during the period of the student
teaching must be obtained from the university supervisor prior to the beginning of the student teaching period.

Role of the Principal

Principals occupy apex positions, and like all high level executives,
they are subject to fierce pressures and stresses. The professional life of
a principal is becoming less satisfying for many. In some areas' the resig-
nation rate of principals has risen; an indication that pressures are not
worth the rewards.

As office holder, the principal is expected to simultaneously perform in
many roles. Some of the roles are traditional, some are easily met and some
are very satisfying. Our roles, their demands and their pressures are part of
the job. Wishing will not make them disappear. If we fail to gain control
over the role shaping process, the outcomes might be severe psychological
stress leading to mental and physical problems.

1. Principal as a Counselor: The principal's work brings him into
contact with some of the most highly motivated and sensitive professionals in
our society - Teachers. These teachers are probably among the most maligned

of all people. The principal comes to the counseling portion of his job equipped with many assets - an education, experience in human relationships and his individual personality.

2. <u>Principal as a Coach</u>: The effective educational leader does differ from the head coach in the way in which he utilizes his team of assistants. Five specific suggestions are as follows:

a. Surround yourself with people who are smarter than you are. The more they know, the better your operation will function and the less likely it is that you will make mistakes.

b. Listen to them. Make it easy for them to talk to you. Don't tell them what the problem is - ask them.

c. Find out what your sub-ordinates can do best. Let them tell you what they want to accomplish: then help them to achieve their goals.

d. Load them with challenge and responsibility.

e. Give them credit for their accomplishments. Let them know that their work is appreciated.

3. <u>The Principal as an influence on student achievement</u>: Much responsibility today is placed on local school system for "producing" student achievement.

a. Principals can provide teachers with inservice training and other staff development opportunities for successful learning experiences.

b. Principals can strive to develop positive working relationships with teachers and demonstrate that they value student achievement highly.

c. Principals can attempt to secure those internal resources which enable teachers to teach more efficiently.

d. Principals can facilitate positive student teacher relations and encourage teachers to place a high value on student achievement.

e. Principals can encourage and support the efforts of teachers to improve student's self-concepts toward higher achievement.

The Role of the Cooperating Teacher

The cooperating teacher plays many roles - director, helper, critic, guide, and others. The student teacher should attempt to work with the cooperating teacher as a junior partner in a common enterprise and to assist him in the various duties in which he engages. Your cooperating teacher is an experienced teacher, has been recommended by his administrators as a master teacher, and is interested in helping you to become a successful teacher. He is assisting you as a cooperating teacher because he is willing to accept and carry out his professional responsibility. Your cooperating teacher is human and makes some errors. Nevertheless, you should respect and assist him wholeheartedly. Remember, one of these years, you may be supervising a student teacher.

The welfare of the students taught by the student teacher is the primary responsibility of the cooperating teacher and the cooperating school. The student teacher should recognize that some decisions may be made by teachers and administrators of the cooperating school which may not (apparently) be in the best interest of the student teacher but may be necessary because they are in the best interest of the students. Any decision involving the student teacher must be made with the welfare of the cooperating school student in mind and no decision should be made which might jeopardize the educational welfare of the children in the school.

Sometimes serious problems may arise between the student teacher and the cooperating teacher. These must be caught and solved in time. There appears to be a natural tendency for some student teachers to hide their problems, to brood about them, and to hope they will go away. When a problem arises for a student teacher, he should discuss it with his cooperating teacher immediately. If the problem is of the type which cannot be discussed with the cooperating teacher, the student teacher should then talk with the principal or notify his university supervisor immediately.

The Role of Other School Personnel

During your student teaching experience you will become acquainted with school employees other than your cooperating teacher. This group includes other faculty members, the custodian, the school secretary and the school librarian. These people are extremely important and can be an invaluable aid to you.

The other faculty members can help student teachers in several ways. Learning about certain students, the philosophy of the school, teaching techniques and methods, and school policies and regulations are just a few items that can be learned by listening and observing other teachers.

If your school has a full-time librarian, that is someone to meet as soon as possible. The librarian will in many schools, be in charge of instructional aids and audio-visual materials and equipment. Their help in choosing the right books, aids, or equipment for a particular lesson or unit can save a lot of time and mistakes.

The other essential group in the school is the secretary and janitor. These two people are important in the every day routine of the school and can make a positive contribution to the school environment. In many cases these people have been in their jobs for several years and are well acquainted with parents, students and faculty. They can help by sharing their general knowledge and experience with you. Always be sure to do more listening than talking, the things you learn about the school, in general, can be very important someday.

In every instance remember that you are training to be a professional teacher. As a student teacher you generate and have access to information that should be considered confidential. It is not ethical to discuss professional matters with other employees in the school. When talking or working with other staff people always remain discreet, but extend to them the same courtesy and cooperation you give to your cooperating teacher.

Role of the University Supervisor

Each student teacher is assigned by the student teaching office or the advisement office to a university supervisor. The University Supervisor is a faculty member who assists in the supervision of several student teachers. Each week he visits the schools to which the student teacher is assigned, consults with the cooperating teacher and the administrator of the cooperating school, holds conferences with the student teacher, and visits the classroom of the student teacher. The university supervisor is the student-teacher's main link with the university during the student teaching period. He helps to make student teaching a worthwhile experience.

Communications are vital during this period, and many conferences are necessary. The student teacher who attempts to operate with a minimum of communication with his cooperating teacher and his university supervisor is courting trouble.

Conferences involving the student teacher and the cooperating teacher should be both formal and informal in nature and should be held frequently during the entire student teaching period. If the university supervisor does not take the initiative in scheduling conferences, the student teacher should ask for a conference appointment. At least one summary conference should be held each week. If the student teacher has a special problem to discuss with the university supervisor he may contact the university supervisor at the university by mail or phone.

It is vital that a formal conference with the university supervisor be scheduled during the middle of the student teaching period. In this conference, the student teacher compares his self-evaluation on the student teacher evaluation form with the cooperating teacher's evaluation using the same form. This procedure promotes a careful appraisal of the characteristics on which the student teacher needs to concentrate to make improvements. Another such formal evaluation converence must be held at the end of the student teaching period.

The Role of the Student Teaching Office

The Student Teaching Office has numerous functions within the Teacher Education Program. They arrange student teaching assignments for all elementary and secondary school majors. These assignments are processed from the application cards which are filed one year in advance. Permits for your student teaching assignment may be picked up in the student teaching office.

The Student Teaching Office also provides instructional materials, and conducts orientation sessions for seniors, cooperating teachers, and university supervisors.

The most time consuming job of the Student Teaching Office is checking to be sure all seniors meet the university requirements for student teaching. They must be sure that all students have been admitted to the Teacher Education Program, that seniors all have a health clearance (a state law) and that all student teachers have an overall grade point of 2.15.

If you have any questions about your student teaching assignment, registration, or requirements, contact this office.

Use of Instructional Material

Lesson Plans - All other things being equal, a lesson that is well planned in advance will be a better lesson. Student teachers, who are in the process of learning how to teach, should expect to spend a great deal more time, effort, and care in planning lessons than experienced teachers.

There is a strong temptation among student teachers to adopt a handicapping set of attitudes toward lesson planning. Because they see experienced teachers planning in more brief form, they deem it unnecessary that they should expend the time and effort required to plan thoroughly. An equally handicapping concept for a student teacher to develop is to view lesson planning as a necessary evil accomplished only to meet the requirements of the university supervisor. In addition to the teacher's plan book, which although adequate for the experienced teacher are usually quite brief, the student teacher is expected to prepare complete, fairly detailed lesson plans for each of the lessons he will teach.

The first few lessons in each new class the student teacher undertakes should be planned co-operatively with the cooperating teacher. Later, the student teacher may take sole responsibility for making up the plan but it should be completed well enough in advance for the cooperating teacher to have an opportunity to check it over and discuss it before it is used in the classroom.

A sample lesson plan form is provided to the student teacher and to the cooperating teacher. This is a suggested form. The format may be revised to fit a particular situation; but the form used should ensure careful, adequate planning of each lesson before it is taught. In certain areas, unit plans may wisely be developed and used; however, proper attention must be given to planning each day's activity. Formal, detailed lesson plannings not only engage the student teacher in a worthwhile job-preparation experience, it also provides the best assurance of instruction, compensating somewhat for the student teacher's lack of teaching experience. The student teacher must remember that some lessons can be taught with a minimum of lesson planning depending on the academic background and experience of the person whereas other lessons will take indepth, detailed lesson plans.

Classroom Management

During the first three years, many teachers "drop out" of teaching and change their profession. Research indicates that over fifty percent of the people who have left the teaching profession during this time left because of classroom management problems and disciplinary techniques. So let's not talk theory but try some practical approaches and applications. Good teaching can only occur in an orderly, wellrun classroom. The teacher is in charge of the room, so the teacher alone is the one who determines whether it is going to be a good place to learn, or merely a poorly run baby sitting service.

You must determine early in your student teaching experience the difference between a noisy noise and a learning or working noise. Your attitude, the very expressing on your face and tone of your voice will tell your students whether you mean business or whether they can push you around. You must never forget you are the leader. You are the adult, the person in charge, the one who the student wants to look up to. Give them someone worth looking up to. In order to do this, you will need to be well organized. This means you must know exactly what you are going to do, when you are going to do it and why. So, first of all, you must be familiar with the daily schedule - what time the tardy bell rings, when recess and lunch hour occur. Do not put yourself in the position of having to ask the students how the school operates. Know yourself so that you can tell them.

From the very first you must be firm but fair; tell the students at once what you expect. How can they know what is acceptable behavior if you don't establish certain definite standards and abide by them? Many years ago I overheard a ten year old boy talking to a friend. He recently transfered from a high permissive school to one which had definite rules of behavior. The friend said, "How do you like it here?" "I hear they are awfully strict." The boy replied, "They are, but I like it because you know what you can do, and just what you can't."

This is security - to know what you may do and what you may not. Consider a moment; how safe would you feel driving a car if the traffic laws changed every day - or if there weren't any at all?

All this does not mean that you must have masses of rules and regulations. Too many rules and regulations are as bad as none. Instead - remember there are two basic reasons for making rules: 1. to ensure the physical safety of the children and 2. to provide an atmosphere conducive for learning. Right at the start set up a definite system for all the routine matter such as: entering the classroom, sharpening pencils, distributing books, collecting papers, and so forth. Having these routine procedures eliminates confusion and disorder that can lead to bedlam - just exactly as having all drivers on the right instead of wherever they want. Having set up these standards, stick to them. You will have to go over them often, but do not compromise. Don't worry if the students call you strict. Over the years, the "strictest" teachers are the ones whose former students return most often for a visit. Help your class to see how everyone benefits from having certain procedures. The majority of the students want to learn, enjoy working, and resent it when a few disturb them. If you permit these few to disrupt the classroom the children will resent and despise you. They look to you as an adult, to provide them with a good place to work.

It is perfectly true that students need more freedom in some situations than in others, but good discipline is not on again - off again. You cannot let children run wild one minute, then expect them to be perfectly controlled to work the next minute.

Planning and organizing are especially important during the first few weeks of school. Never start anything new, no matter how obvious it may appear (even something that seems as simple as passing out textbooks or taking a bathroom break) without first planning with your group how it's going to be done. Don't worry if it seems you're spending a lot of time setting the stage at first. It will pay big dividends later. Once acceptable standards of behavior are established you will be able to cover the academic material more rapidly and more thoroughly than you ever dreamed possible.

As soon as possible you want to get to know your students. Learn their names, study their records, so that you will know their weaknesses and their strengths and be better able to help them. Find out about their abilities and their problems. But don't ever forget that you are their teacher - you are their friend but not their buddy. They need a contempory for a buddy - they want a teacher to admire, to respect, to model, and to emulate.

Organization and planning are essential for good discipline and it bears repeating that the organization of time and activities are essential! Also one must organize space and facilities. Your room arrangement can help mean good discipline. Separating the trouble-makers is, of course, the most obvious tactic, but there is more to letting your room arrangement help you than just that.

Naturally, the first factor you have to consider is safety. Are the aisles at least thirty inches wide? Is there clear access to the exits in case of emergency? Is the furniture so arranged that no desk, chair or wastebasket is a barricade to traffic? Is there easy access to those items frequently

used - pencil sharpener, waste-basket, reference books? Are your aisles kept

clear of books and feet so that it is possible to move around safety and

quietly? And don't forget the effect that the appearance of your room has on

the class. A neat room, with attractive bulletin boards and tidy book shelves

is more conducive to work than a sloppy room. And if students are working they

are not misbehaving. So establish working areas and learning center areas.

In order to have good control of your students, you must be aware at all

times what is going on. The teacher who sits at her desk to teach limits her

effectiveness, and invites trouble. Whenever you work with a class as a whole,

you should have to work hard to get and retain their undivided attention.

You have to see, to relate, to move around and to use a variety of instruc-

tional materials. You can not do this effectively at your desk. Furthermore,

the alert teacher, moving around the class, can nip in the bud any potential

mischief, thus protecting the class from disturbing interruptions.

The best way to have a successful working day is to start it right. Be

in your room before the class starts. Your presence and friendly but busi-

ness like attitude can work wonders in reminding students that the classroom

is a place to study. Have an assignment on the board so that as soon as they

hang up their coats they can go directly to their seats and get started. In-

sist upon this. Then, when the tardy bell rings, your class is quiet and

relaxed, and ready for the opening exercise. At recess or the end of the day,

don't beat your students out of the door. Aside from the poor example you set,

this is a critical period for accidents and discipline. Take your time and stay in control.

Just remember that your classroom is going to be exactly what you make it! If your standards are high - if you give and demand courtesy and consideration, industry and efficiency, orderliness and organization, that is exactly what you will get.

So in facing the problems of classroom management and discipline one must be alert and active and "see everything" and must employ a wide attention range.

It is essential to walk around the room, talk to individuals, smile at the students, ask them questions but not be too obvious in your motives. A good sense of humor of the light laughter type will help establish rapport with the students. You must treat each student with respect as though he were the son or daughter of the most prominent person in the community. It is helpful to make a seating chart and have an information card on each student. If you know all their names, hobbies, interests, and their habits, you will find that by talking with them informally you will get to know each one as an individual and be able to treat that person with respect.

The teacher must be sincere and well-meaning. You will have to be stern, happy, firm, informal, kindly, unrelenting and so forth. To protect the integrity of your own emotional pattern act appropriately and sincerely. Be self-confident and have courage and moral convictions. Things that will help include thoroughly prepared plans, plenty of sleep, recreation in a non-school circle, allowing the students to help with heat, lights, air, attendance, books, bulletin boards, committees, and so forth.

See your students somewhere else than in the classroom. Look at them

44

on the athletic field, in music, or art programs, during recess, at committee meetings, at school parties and so forth. You must maintain an adult reserve teacher-student relationship, a formality whereby the students know there will be no popularity play and no siding with the students against other teachers or administrators. You must be very careful not to have favorites or crushes on any particular student. Another indication of respect is that the students call you Miss, Ms., Mrs., or Mr., not ever by just your first or last name.

Be just and very fair with students; try to put yourself in their place. Follow the "golden rule" and/or the old Indian saying which is "to put your-self in their moccasins so you can see with their eyes what they see and better understand them."

In disciplinary situations suspend your judgement; often be impersonal and sometimes you must even be coldly nonchalant. It is not necessary to settle every case. You are not dealing with the psychology nor the logic of the situation. When you are in error, say you are in error, and be ready to apologize. But try not to be in error often.

Be enthusiastic about your field and this will kindle a response from your students. Do nothing yourself that you can get students to do even though they do it less effectively; the schooling is for them, and they like to help. Encourage but do not scold students who do poorly. There is usually something you can find to compliment them, even if it is a sharpened pencil or well combed hair.

Create situations where you share problems with children. They like nothing better than the question, "What shall we do about this?" Try never to become angry. To activate adrenals means mental confusion; lower your voice, grow impressive, but avoid a scene; after all, it is a professional not a personal matter. Do everything you can to build up the ego of each student, by assigning jobs, honoring the student, or give a kindly compliment, or a smile - all these things count more in children's lives than most teachers realize. Use your voice effectively; it can sooth when lowered, enthuse when the tones are rich and the range is wide; it can accentuate bedlam when it tries to shout.

Every once in a while do something for the class yourself with an air that you are happy and you are trying to please them. Read to them, show them a clipping, tell an interesting personal experience, all to make them feel secure, important, and that you care for them. Try to avoid creating a situation where students have to lie, and above all else let them save face when you know they are in a tight spot. Teach them something they really want to know. Have something ready for them. Make interesting environments in the room. Have good magazines about, books with attractive jackets, pictures, flowers, various learning center areas. This will encourage students to read books, to investigate, to be involved.

Discuss problems with children but never lecture. Remember your own experience and never try to talk louder than the whole class. Talk quietly and talk to individuals. When you are uncertain what to do about a class situation or an individual case simply ask yourself what "common sense" would suggest. You will be surprised at the simplicity of the solution. When you give directions, let them be clear and concise: say them aloud distinctly while you are looking into a selection of students' eyes; write them out, underlining with yellow chalk parts to be noted particularly and then ask several students to tell you what they mean. Take nothing for granted. Above all else ask, "and why are we doing this?" If there is no intelligent answer, select a different task.

You must have plans ready when the class begins. Never tie yourself up by having to put material on the board or look up references while the students are in circulation. If you are in the school for the first time, perhaps for the day as a substitute, make a quick survey of the educational flavor of the place. You can always tell from the initial greeting, the books and other educational items in the room. Stay alert.

If a new class stages "a revolt," sit down with them, drop your own book, laugh with them and relax with them. Take the matter lightly in stride and they will soon swear by you. This is better than glaring and fear! Keep "twenty jumps" ahead of the students at all times.

When the class is at work avoid interruptions at all times, but comment to individual students. Leave the students alone to work because constant interruptions from teachers are distracting.

It might be well to look at the following items and have in mind at least five things that you can think through carefully when classroom management problems arise. For example, do you have interesting work for the students? Can you talk to them? Can you take away privileges? Can you see the student on his own time, i.e. after school? Can you have him write an agreement that he will honor with you or with the principal? Can you phone or write a note to the parents? Can you ask the parents to visit the class? Can you visit

the home? Do you have all the personal data from the counselor and other

special teachers that would help you in watching and working with a particular

"problem" student? Can you learn to overlook some things? Do you make an

appointment or send the child to see the principal as a last resort?

So in establishing guidelines and rules, you must involve the class and

the guidelines must be short and to the point. All rules should be phrased

in a positive way and should vary for different activities. The teacher should

call attention and discuss rules and regulations other than just when someone

"misbehaves." The rules should be posted in a conspicuous location and you

should keep a personal record of the number of times you discuss or comment

on this short list of rules.

A characteristic of disciplinary action is that it should always have as

its prime consideration that of aiding the students to better self-control. It

must be related to the misbehavior and be fair, just, and consistant. The

teacher must remain impersonal yet be constructive and not arouse fear in the

child. The teacher must not involve the disciplinary action in assigning extra

work that is unrelated to the act for which the student is being punished.

Effective discipline must be divided into several areas. These areas

would include getting off to the right start at the beginning of the year with

the organized routines that we have previously discussed by letting the class

know exactly what you expect of them.

Another awareness should be at the start of the day when the children

enter the room. This will help form good work habits and avoid problems for the rest of the day. The appearance of the room of course has a great deal

to do with classroom management and discipline. If the room is a stimulating,

attractive place the students tend to gear their behavior accordingly. If the

place is "trashy-unorganized" the children tend to act accordingly.

Another area of concern is children who arrive late or continually want

to go to the bathroom or the learning center or some other area. If you have

set procedures you can avoid many problems in the hallways and the lavoratories.

The same applies on the playground and at lunch time. One must remember that

we need to teach good manners at all times and be especially aware of each

child as an individual who has unique rights and responsibilities.

Some specific suggestions are:

1. Be active and alert. "See everything." Employ a wide attention

range.

2. Walk around. Talk to individuals. Smile at pupils. Ask them plea-

sant questions. Do not be too obvious in your motives.

3. Cultivate and use your sense of humor. Not the bread-joke type,

but the light-touch-laughter type.

4. Treat each pupil as though he were the mayor's son or daughter. Be

more than usually courteous to your attendance law prisoners.

5. Make a seating chart and have an information card for each pupil.

Know all names, hobbies, interests, domestic habits of each student. Find out

these things by talking informally subtly, recording the information later.

6. Learn to act, sincerely and well. Bette Davis does it; you will have

to be stern, happy, firm, informal; kindly, unrelenting; etc. To protect the

49

integrity of your own emotional pattern, learn to act appropriately and sincerely.

7. _Be self-confident_. Have courage, moral courage to face the situation. It may be hard to appear self-confident, but it is a first essential. These things will help: prepared plans, sleep, recreation in non-school circles, using pupils to help with heat, lights, air, attendance, books, bulletin boards, committees, etc. If you cannot "take it" look for a more pleasant occupation.

8. _"See" your pupils somewhere else than in the classroom_. In the school, on the athletic field, on the noon playground, at the student council, at the school parties, etc.

9. _Keep an adult reserve of formality which the pupils know is there_. No playing for popularity, no siding with pupils against other teachers or administration, with the students, never _of_ them; no favorites, crushes; always Miss, Mrs., or Mr., never just Smith.

10. _Be just, very fair_. Put yourself in the pupil's place. The Golden Rule. What shape would you be in without sleep, food or security.

11. _In disciplinary situations suspend your judgment, often be impersonal sometimes even coldly nonchalant_. It is not necessary to settle every case. You are dealing with the psychology not the logic of the situation.

12. _Say so when you are in error_. Even be ready to apologize - but not too often.

13. _Be enthusiastic about your field_. And it will kindle responses in your pupils.

14. _Do nothing yourself that you can get pupils to do_. Even though they do it less effectively; the schooling is for them, they like to help.

15. Encourage. Not scold when pupils do poorly. There is usually something you can find to compliment, even a sharp pencil or well combed hair.

16. Create "a learning emergency" in which you share a problem with pupils;
they like nothing better; e.g. "What shall we do about this?"

17. Try never to become angry. To active adrenals mean mental confusion;
lower your voice, grow impressive, but avoid a scene; after all, it is a
professional, not a personal matter.

18. Do everything that you can to build up the ego of each pupil. Jobs,
honors, a kindly compliment; a smile - all count more in the pupil's lives
than we realize.

19. Use your voice effectively. It can soothe when lowered, enthuse
when the tones are rich and the range of pitch is wide; it can accentuate
bedlam when it tries to out shout it.

20. Every once in a while do something for the class yourself with an air
that you are happy to please them. Read to them, show them a clipping; tell
an interesting personal experience - all to make them feel cared for.

21. Try to avoid creating a situation where pupils have to lie. Above
all, let them save face when you know they are in a tight spot.

22. Teach them something. They really want it. Have something ready for
them.

23. Make an interesting environment of the room with the help of the pupils.
Have good magazines about, books with attractive jackets, pictures, flowers,
etc.

24. Encourage pupils to have a library book to fill in spare moments or

to relieve the strain of working too long on one thing.

25. <u>Discuss problems with pupils, but never "lecture".</u> Remember your
own faculty meeting experiences. See how little you can talk out loud to the
whole class. Get in your licks by talking quietly to individuals.

26. <u>When you are uncertain what to do about a class situation or an
individual case</u> simply ask yourself what common sense would suggest. You will
be surprised at the simplicity of the solutions.

27. <u>When you give directions.</u> Let them be clear and concise: say them
out loud distinctly while you look into a selection of pupil's eyes; write
them out, underlining with yellow chalk the parts to be noted particularly;
then ask several pupils to tell what they mean. Take nothing for granted.
Above all, ask, "And why are we doing this?" If there is no intelligent answer,
select a different task.

28. <u>Have your own plans ready when the class beings.</u> Never tie yourself
up to having to put material on the board during class time; pupils will do
it while you are in circulation.

29. <u>If you are in the school for the first time</u> and perhaps just for the
day, make a quick survey of the educational flavor of the place; there are ways
to tell: the initial office greeting, the books in the teachers' library, the
decorations, the restroom and luncheon talk. Say little, alertly observe.

30. <u>If a new class stages "a revolt in a tea cup"</u> sit down with them,
drop your own book; laugh with them and say you get paid for it. Take the
matter lightly in stride and they will soon swear by you. Better than glaring
and fear! Keep "twenty jumps" ahead of the students.

31. <u>When you have set a class at work, avoid interrupting them by across-the-room comments to the individuals.</u> Leave them alone; pupils find constant interruptions by the teacher distracting.

32. Make a check list of disciplinary measures that should be exhausted before sending the "case" pupil to the office. For example:

give interesting work to do

talk with him

take away privileges

see him on his time

check with his homeroom teacher

"exercise the brute" by sending him on an errand or asking the physical education instructor to permit an additional workout

have him write an agreement which he must get the homeroom teacher, vice principal and perhaps parents to sign

phone or write a note to parents

ask parents to visit his class

visit the home

get all the personal data from counselor and homeroom teacher

go with him on appointment to the principal for a conference

do something nice, but unaffected, for the "case" to show you hold no ill will

learn to apparently not see everything

Legal Aspects of Teaching

There are a few terms that each teacher must be aware of even though the school district usually pays the court cost and the judgement if a teacher is sued. One of these terms is Loco Parentus which means in place of the parent or assumes the role of the parents. In other words the teachers have the right to make certain rules for good order and discipline. The teacher must act in good faith and of course use "common sense." For example, in Pennsylvania there was a court case where a teacher held a child's infected finger under hot water and, not realizing the temperature of the water, burned the child severely. In his case the teacher was liable.

Tort is the right of personal security, the right of ownership of property, and the right to enjoy a good reputation. This can either be private or civil and protects the teacher against personal injury, trespass upon anothers property, defamation of character, and the maintenance of a nuisance.

Foreseeability simply means that if the teacher can foresee what is going to happen they can be held liable.

Negligence is the failure to exercise reasonable or ordinary care. For example, when on field trips the teacher must be aware that the children do not have knives or instruments that might harm another child. The same applies in the classroom. Negligence might be found if there are extremely frayed electrical cords or connections, if proper care is not taken in the use of chemicals, or industrial arts equipment as well as in mismatching of either little boys or little girls against big boys or girls in Physical Education.

Save harmless for years protected school districts and teachers against being sued by parents or someone in the community. However, in the case of Molitar vs. Kaneland the statute was reversed and a school can be sued. So with this landmark decision teachers must be more aware of their legal rights and responsibilities.

As the population expands and the culture continues to become more complex there are more concerns for health, education and welfare of children. The average citizen is more legal conscious and we are finding now that "everybody" files lawsuits. Insurance rates for liability have increased tremendously in the last few years and in the case of the medical profession some doctors have quit the profession because of law suits and the amount of money spent on insurance. It appears that teachers will have more and more law suits filed against them as we continue to have teacher strikes, contract negotiations, and continual collective bargaining.

The Supreme Court decisions have had a direct affect on teachers beginning with the 1954 decision requiring desegregation of the public schools that was filed by Brown vs. the Board of Education. Other important decisions were banning prayer in public schools (Engle vs. Vitale) in 1962, and the decision prohibiting the devotional use of the Bible in public schools (school district of Abbington Township vs. Schempp; Murray vs. Curlett) in 1963.

Teachers must be very aware of the punishment laws in their state and the policies of their individual school district. For example, in Illinois there is no state law against punishment but a variety of districts have school policy which would not permit a teacher to "strike" a child. One must be very aware that any punishment must be according to the offense. One must consider the age, the sex, the condition of the child, and be sure that punishment is being used for what the child has done and not as a result of the teacher's anger. In other words, the action of the child should have been realized and he should understand why he is being punished.

There are many statutory laws in each state as well as case laws. The case law sets precedent and is usually based on an individual case. Statutory laws usually are individual state laws. The National Reporter System lists all court cases. One should be aware that these are listed by section and that the beginning teacher may obtain this list for his section to see what type of cases have appeared in the courts in recent years. Teachers have been found guilty, so be careful!

Most school districts carry liability insurance but the teacher should carefully investigate on his own. For example, the State Education Association as well as the National Education Association usually carries liability insurance. So for a modest sum teachers may obtain personal liability insurance. There have been a variety of court cases, some of which will be discussed briefly here so that you will be aware of the various types of lawsuits that have been filed. Fertich vs. Michener - this case was concerned with outside doors of the school being locked in very cold weather and the children not permitted to come inside. Reasonable rules here must apply and if the weather is severely cold the students must be permitted to come inside the building.

Mitchell vs. McCall - this case involved gym dress for girls where one family felt that the gym dress was immodest.

Leonard vs. school committee of Atteboro - this involved extreme haircuts for boys who were wearing long hair.

Strombert vs. French - this case dealt with the student wearing metal heal plates and the school maintained that damage was being done to the floors as well as noise and confusion caused by the student wearing excessively large metal plates on his shoes.

Pugsley vs. Selalmyer was a case involving immodest wearing of face paint and cosmetics by a lower elementary girl. So we must be very concerned about student dress.

In the State of Indiana vs. Vanderbilt as well as cases in other states the case law set precedent that parents are financially responsible for damage or destruction of school property by their children.

Flory vs. Smith case was concerned with students leaving the school premises during lunch hour. The case was built around a child who would have had to eat a cold meal if she were not permitted to go home.

McLane Independent School District vs. Andrews concerns students driving during the lunch hour. The school's policy was to require cars to be parked and not driven during the day. The student who drove the car during the lunch hour was in an accident and was injured. The school was sued for not enforcing the policy of not permitting the students driving except to and from school.

There have been a number of cases, one as early as 1929, concerning student marriage and expulsion because of marriage. The courts have ruled that students may not be excluded because 1. marriage is a domestic relation highly favored by law, 2. married students might desire to further their education, 3. married students must not be denied the right to public school education. Schools can however limit extracurricular activities of married students. Student pregnancy is another area of concern and the courts have ruled that students have to withdraw but the school must continue the education through a home-studies program.

Many states have laws prohibiting student membership in secret societies and students in these states can be expelled if they are holding secret memberships. However most states remain silent on this issue.

The courts have ruled that students can be punished for actions off the school grounds and after school hours if it has a direct effect on discipline, morale, or the good order of the school. Other court cases include bullying of students on their way to school or on their way home from school, being drunk and disorderly, smoking cigarettes, using drugs, failing to obey the principal or superintendent and so forth.

Rules in a school must be reasonable and the enforcement of these rules must be reasonable. Privileges can be withheld, students can be removed from the classroom, and students can be sent home if there are no unreasonable hazards involved. The courts have ruled unfavorably for schools using academic punishment for disciplinare infractions, grade reductions for disciplinary infractions and withholding of diplomas for disciplinary infractions.

The teacher must then check very carefully the expulsion and suspension rules of the district and the policies of their particular school. Suspension is usually defined as an exclusion from school for a specified brief period of time and expulsion is for a longer length of time, a semester or perhaps a school year. Expulsion should involve school board action.

There have been many cases dealing with corporal or physical punishment of students. Some states expressly permit corporal punishment by statute.

There have been cases of faculty involved in dress code. For example, one school faculty got together and decided to wear frayed blue jeans, tight blouses, pullovers without brassieres, and so on, and the court ruled against them. So you must know your legal liabilities and your responsibilities.

CHAPTER 4

FORMS AND RECORDS

Personal Data Forms

There are several types of student personal data forms used by various colleges and universities to convey and record a maximum of background information about the student teacher. This form should be completed by the student teacher early in the professional semester, well before the student teaching period, so that the university supervisor and the cooperating teacher can acquire a basic orientation to the student teacher before he is assigned to the school and grade level of teaching.

After the student teaching period begins it should be placed in the student's folder for future reference and conferences. This then would become part of the permanent file for the student teacher which would be maintained by the university supervisor or by the counseling-advising office.

Some universities use a student teacher weekly report which is mailed to the university supervisor at the end of each week during the student teaching period, to arrive on the university supervisor's desk by Monday of the following week. It conveys information about the previous week's work and general plans for the coming week, and information that is useful in scheduling the visits of the university supervisor. As an incidental outcome it encourages the student teacher to focus sharply on the continuity of his plans and actions from one week to the next. This report can become part of the student's folder as well as being used by the university supervisor.

Another form which is used by many universities is the Absent From Student Teaching form. This form is to be used in case a student attends a funeral, or is seriously ill and will be out for several days or is interviewing for a job. The student teacher simply requests permission to be absent from the student teaching position so the cooperating teacher can continue with planned activities. The university supervisor must be informed so he will not make a special trip to observe while the student is absent. Another form is used if the student is absent due to an illness of short duration.

Other records that are expected to be completed by the student teacher should be done in a very proper, accurate, and useful way. Usually these have to do with student progress, attendance, and various other clerical activities. The student teacher is expected to adjust to the record keeping procedure of the cooperating teacher and the cooperating school.

There are a variety of forms used to request media equipment, films, and other curricular library materials. The student teacher is expected to use a variety of materials to stimulate interest and participation in the topic and to enrich the school program.

The student teacher is to maintain a series of folders on lesson plans, evaluation techniques, student records, and similar material for the cooperating teacher and university supervisor. The folder should be kept in a place where it is available to both student teacher and cooperating teacher so that there is a good means of communication between them.

It is well to maintain this folder and give it to the university supervisor prior to the writing of the final evaluation. If the folder contains the personal data record, samples of (used) lesson plans, and samples of other course materials used as well as the mid-term self-evaluation sheets and other items specified by the university supervisor, it will aid the university supervisor in writing his final evaluation.

Student Teacher Evaluation Forms

Student teaching evaluation forms serve as a summary evaluation of the student teacher by the cooperating teacher and the university supervisor. In addition, it is strongly urged that the student teacher self-evaluate his own experiences and abilities. The forms contain group categories of characteristics important in considering growth and achievement of the student teacher. The form is set up as a check list which identifies individual characteristics to be evaluated separately on a value scale and then a brief, pertinent comment entered in paragraph form to support the categories and elaborate on the student's performance.

A mid-term evaluation form based on the check list but used informally will help the student teacher in assessing his performance and is a good communication with the cooperating teacher and the university supervisor. Mid-term evaluations are never recorded and a student then has an opportunity to grow and achieve in the areas of concern. The cooperating teacher and the university supervisor should sit down with the student teacher in informal conference both for the mid-term and the final evaluation and discuss carefully the ratings and the narrative description of the student teacher which is placed in the placement file.

There are a number of evaluation forms and techniques but the following form grew out of over two years work by various committees including elementary school teachers, administrators, university teachers and administrators. There was a strong feeling that the narrative describing each classification be attached so that the student teacher, the cooperating teacher, and the university supervisor each had common grounds for evaluation. It is also suggested that copies of this form be provided to the placement office to be included in the placement file so that hiring officials have an opportunity to understand and critically evaluate the recommendations both from the check list and the narrative.

ELEMENTARY STUDENT TEACHING
Northern Illinois University

MID-TERM REPORT OF TEACHING ABILITY

This is an advance estimate of the ability of the teacher candidate who is
presently student teaching. Please check items with appropriate numbers. At
the end of the student teaching assignment another sheet will be forwarded to
you which will later go to the placement office.

NAME_____School_____
Subjects Taught_____Grade Level_____

Rating: Place an "X" at the point of the continuum that indicates your
          appraisal of the student teacher in each of the categories listed.*

Outstanding: consistently superior   Satisfactory: fulfilling all requirements
Needs Improvement: lacks proficiency and/or experience
Insufficient Evidence: little or no basis for judgment

	O	S	NI	IE			O	S	NI	IE
1. Methods of instruction						11. Adaptability				
2. Knowledge of subject						12. Dependability				
3. Organizing and Planning						13. Initiative				
4. Classroom control						14. Enthusiasm				
5. Ability to motivate						15. Use of English				
6. Attitude toward students						16. Emotional maturity				
7. Ability to communicate						17. Sense of humor				
8. Evaluation of students						18. Speech & Voice				
9. Creativity						19. Tact				
10. Cooperation						20. Professionalism				

General statement concerning student teacher's work:

The student shows promise of becoming a: Good_____Fair_____Poor_____Teacher.

_____
Supervising Classroom Teacher

*For interpretation of categories, please see Competency Based Criteria for
Student Teachers.

64

NORTHERN ILLINOIS UNIVERSITY
Student Teaching Record

Pursuant to Public Law 93-380 references written on 11/19/74 or after are open for inspection by the candidates

CAREER PLANNING AND PLACEMENT

NAME_____ SCHOOL_____

SCHOOL ADDRESS_____ DATES TAUGHT_____

SUBJECTS TAUGHT_____ GRADE LEVEL_____

Rating: Place an "X" at the point of the continuum that indicates your appraisal of the student teacher in each of the categories listed.

Outstanding: consistently superior   Satisfactory: fulfilling all requirements
Needs Improvement: lacks proficiency and/or experience
Insufficient Evidence: little or no basis for judgment

	O	S	NI	IE			O	S	NI	IE
1. Methods of instruction					11. Adaptability					
2. Knowledge of subject					12. Dependability					
3. Organizing & planning					13. Initiative					
4. Classroom control					14. Enthusiasm					
5. Ability to motivate					15. Use of English					
6. Attitude toward students					16. Emotional maturity					
7. Ability to communicate					17. Sense of humor					
8. Evaluation of students					18. Speech and voice					
9. Creativity					19. Tact					
10. Cooperation					20. Professionalism					

Summarizing Statements: (Please mention specific strengths and weaknesses as well as potential success as a teacher.)

_____   _____Supervising Classroom Teacher
(Signature)

_____   _____University Supervisor
(Typed Name)

_____
(Date)

Evaluation of the University Supervisor by Students

Some university professors wish to obtain an evaluation of their teaching effectiveness from their students. The university can either recommend or discourage this practice and leave the decision to the discretion of the university professor and the student teacher. If the university professor wishes to obtain any evaluation - by - students, he should have the approval of the university.

Suggestions would include: a. insist upon anonymity of responses - no names on papers, all marked in pencil, the papers shuffled upon being collected. b. use a checklist type reading sheet. Allow no essay - type comments; these can contain certain uncomplimentary comparisons. c. follow through on the evaluating by tabulating the responses, analyzing the results and discussing possible improvements with your supervising teacher. You must justify the student - time spent on this activity by the improvement that it will help you make in your instruction.

A sample form for student evaluation:

NORTHERN ILLINOIS UNIVERSITY
DeKalb, Illinois

SURVEY OF STUDENT OPINION OF TEACHING

PLEASE FOLLOW THESE DIRECTIONS:

A. Read the description of the qualities listed.
B. Mark one of the numbers indicating the rating of your present instructor.
C. Do this in each of the qualities under the heading "Instructor".
D. MAKE EACH ANSWER A SEPARATE JUDGEMENT.

....

INSTRUCTOR	LOW				HIGH
Knowledge of his subject	1	2	3	4	5
Skill in presenting subject	1	2	3	4	5
Interest and enthusiasm in subject	1	2	3	4	5
Tolerance & emotional balance	1	2	3	4	5
Helpfulness to students	1	2	3	4	5
Sense of humor	1	2	3	4	5
Freedom from annoying mannerisms	1	2	3	4	5

Would you recommend the instructor for
tenure?   Yes_____   No_____

The instructor earned my respect   Yes_____   No_____

Would you recommend the instructor
to teach this class again?   Yes_____   No_____

Was the instructor available before and
after class in his office or by phone?   Yes_____   No_____

List positive aspects of the <u>class</u>:

List positive aspects of the <u>instructor</u>:

List negative aspects of the <u>class</u>:

List negative aspects of the <u>instructor</u> (things that bothered you):

Marks in Student Teaching

Honest, accurate marks are probably more difficult to assign in student teaching than in any other college teacher education course. There is a strong emotional identification of the individual teacher's self with the mark he receives in this important course. Evaluation of student teaching is necessarily highly subjective since the teaching task defies the mechanical restriction necessary to obtain objectivity. Since it is so highly subjective, there is always a strong possibility for human error. This possibility is recognized and accepted by professional educators, and student teachers should recognize and accept this also.

The system of determining student's marks can either be P-F, S-U, or A, B, C, D, or F, as determined by the university policy on grading.

The final mark should be focused on predicting the probable success of the student teacher in the teaching field. In determining the mark, the university should draw upon all available information in rating sheets, visitation check lists, and reports, both written and oral, submitted by the student teacher, the cooperating teacher, and the principal.

If the P-F marks are used for Pass or Fail and the S-U system of marks is used to indicate that the student is satisfactory or unsatisfactory; it appears that formal assignment of the letter grade A, B, C, D, or F, is more meaningful and would support the evaluation checklist and the paragraph written by the cooperating teacher and the university supervisor.

A general description of the marks of student teaching could include: A's will be assigned to outstanding, excellent, superior student teachers.

B's will be assigned to the above average student teacher with no single significant deficiency. C's will be assigned to all average student teachers. This will include those students who may be above average or have characteristics of one or more significant deficiencies - incorrect grammar; shakey classroom control; monotonous, unimaginative lessons; insufficient background in preparation; so on, so forth. D's will be assigned to those who are likely to have serious difficulty in the teaching field for any combination of two or more demonstrable reasons. F's will be assigned to student teachers whose deficiency is such that they would be a severe liability to the profession and to their potential students.

Forms for the Job Market

Finding your first teaching job is more than just luck. During your student teaching experience, you should be making careful plans to locate your first teaching assignment. The aggressive and enthusiastic prospective teacher will have a good chance to secure a teaching position.

The first step is to prepare your credentials. The Career Planning and Placement Office at NIU has specific forms to begin your credential file. In addition to their forms, you should have your transcript, the evaluation form from your cooperating teacher, an evaluation form from your university supervisor, and two letters of reference. The placement office suggests that this file be prepared early in your final semester so that it may be activated for the next year.

Having a good resume is also a vital part of your credentials. When making out your resume follow an accepted form. There are numerous types available. When you send out your inquiry letters, applications or resume, be sure they are neat, organized, and personal. It is recommended that anything you send out be neatly typed.

The interview will be the most important step in obtaining a teaching position, but the credentials you file with a school district play a major role in obtaining that first interview. To help you become familiar with the forms and records of your credential file, several have been outlined.

SAMPLE LETTER OF APPLICATION

                                    1801 Van Atta Drive
                                    Duluth, Minnesota
                                    February 12, 19__

Mr. Alfred P. Knapp
Superintendent of Schools
New Memorial High School
Duluth, Minnesota

Dear Mr. Knapp:

REASON

    Yesterday Dr. James Parker, the head of the Chemistry Department, told me that you are seeking another science teacher, and he suggested that I apply for the position. Please consider me an applicant.

YOUR STRENGTHS

    I am a graduate of State College and while a student there, I won honors in chemistry and was graduated with honor. I also participated in extracurricular activities and have held two elective offices in campus organizations. During summer vacations I have been employed at the Pleasantville State Fisheries as a laboratory assistant, as a chemist's assistant for the Lederic Laboratory, and last summer I worked as a nature study counselor at a camp for boys. All of this experience has contributed to an ability to get along with other people and to adjust to different situations.

AVAILABILITY

    The enclosed data sheet will give you further details of my personal qualifications and training. I am available for an interview at your convenience.

                                    Very truly yours,

                                    George Patton Hines

Enclosure

PERSONAL DATA SHEET
Georgia Hines
1801 Van Atta Drive
Duluth, Minnesota
Valley 3-7808

Employment desired

I would prefer to teach in one of the intermediate level grades of the elementary school, but I am willing to accept an appointment to any one of the primary level grades.

Personal Data

Age: 21
Height: 5'6"

Weight: 118
Marital Status: Single; to be married in June

Education

Central High School, Duluth, Minnesota (Salutatorian)
State College, Duluth, Minnesota (Honor Student)
    Major: Elementary Education
    Minor: Biology

Extracurricular Activity

Student Council President
Biology Club President
Future Teachers of America Secretary
Member of Tennis Team
School Newspaper Photographer

References

Refer to State College Placement Office

Hobbies

Photography, camping, sports (tennis, bowling)

Work Experience

Summer, 19__   Marlowe Settlement House, Columbia, Minnesota, Assistant Group Leader
Summer, 19__   Windsor Girls' Camp, Burlington, Vermont, Photography and Athletics Counselor
Summer, 19__   Artizan Photography Studio, Duluth, Minnesota Receptionist and Photographer
Spring, 19__   Morgan Elementary School, Duluth, Minnesota Student Teacher - second and fourth grades

RESUMES AND COVER LETTERS
Excerpt from the Job Hunter's Guide

THE RESUME, OR THIS IS YOUR LIFE

In many cases, your resume will be your first contact with an employer. Since the main function of the resume is to get you an interview, always select information which will show you to best advantage. Your resume must adequately promote what you have to offer and create sufficient interest in you for the employer to invite you in for an interview. The following items are found in one form or another in most resumes:

Identifying Information. Your name, current address, and telephone number should be included. Be sure that a permanent address is also listed if you plan to move after graduation.

Job Objective. This may be included on the resume or in the accompanying cover letter, discussed later. There are three points to take into consideration here: Be humble. Employers think that because you are inexperienced, you still have a lot to learn. Be motivated. Try to imply that you are willing to put out superhuman effort for the good of the company. Be appropriately vague. Since you probably don't really know what every job entails, don't limit your chances by appearing to be too specific. However, if you are applying for a specific position that you know is open, be certain to state your objective in a way that relates directly to that position.

Objective: To utilize my background in marketing and my ability to work hard to achieve a position where I can contribute to the sales growth of a company.

Objective: To join a management training program which will enable me to prepare myself for a responsible position in management.

Educational Background. Start with your highest or most recent degree and work back from there. If you had any special emphasis in your studies that you feel contributes toward your objective, mention it. If you feel your grade point average is worthy of attention, include it also. Be sure to indicate whether it is based on a 4 or 5 point scale. If you have received any special academic awards, or have been an officer in a student organization, a member of an athletic team, or so forth, list this also. You may wish to state the percentage of college expenses you earned as well.

Experience or Work History. This is a summary of your work experience emphasizing your most recent or most important job. It describes the nature of your work, the title of your positions, names of employers, and the dates you were employed. This section should not be an obituary of what you have done, but rather an active statement of what you can do.

If you don't have experience directly related to your job objective, don't be too concerned; you are in a majority. What you want to do, though, is to stress the responsibility, achievement, and ability to get the job done that you have demonstrated in your past jobs.

| Sept. 1973 to May 1974 | Assistant Night Manager, McDonald's, DeKalb, IL. Had full responsibility for restaurant two nights each week. |

Now let's rewrite this "obituary entry" so that it shows what you can do for the firm to which you are applying:

| Sept. 1973 to May 1974 | I was the Assistant Night Manager of the McDonald's franchise in DeKalb while a senior. This experience indicates that I am a responsible individual who can maintain careful and accurate records; we had neither cash nor inventory shortages during the nights that I worked. |

Possibly you are applying for a teaching position or some other type of supervisory position. You might take the same job and write it up as:

| Sept. 1973 to May 1974 | I was the Assistant Night Manager for the McDonald's franchise in DeKalb while a senior. From this experience I learned that I can work well with people and can get them to work together for a common purpose; I kept a part-time staff working as a team. We had neither cash nor inventory shortages during the nights I was on duty. |

Military Record. If you have served in the military you may include a brief statement of your military experience in terms a layman can understand. If your work history and educational background were mostly military, then include your military experience and training under those headings.

Activities & Interests. This section helps to give the employer a better developed picture of the total you by giving information about your professional and community affiliations, club memberships, hobbies, and other interests.

Personal Data. Under this category come such things as age, height, weight, marital status, number of children, and health. Information of this type cannot be solicited by an employer in the application process (unless it comprises bona fide occupational requirements), but may be voluntarily provided by you if you feel it is to your advantage. Such things as salary, location, clerical skills and pictures are also optional and should be included only if you feel it would benefit your cause. The location of this material in your resume depends on the format and on how much information you list. It can be listed under a separate heading or be worked into other sections of the resume. The key issue is whether you feel that the inclusion of this information will enhance or detract from your application.

References. You need only state something to the effect that "references are available on request" on your resume. For your own use you should have a list with names, addresses, and telephone numbers of three or four people who will provide good references for you. It is a good idea to bring this list and a copy of your transcript to the interview just in case you are asked about either. Be sure to check with these people beforehand and get their permission to use their names as references.

CHOOSING THE APPROPRIATE FORMAT

The format of your resume is the combination of approach and typographical layout you select for presenting the facts about yourself. If at all possible, the job hunter without related work experience should restrict the length of the resume to one page. This length assures proper coverage, yet increases the probability that the resume will be read. Your approach will naturally dictate the pattern of the typographical layout so your first decision will have to be where to place the emphasis in interpreting your qualifications.

Will you stress how you have spent your time? Or the kind of education you have had? or the skills and abilities you have acquired? or your personal potentials? Here are some descriptions of the most common approaches.

Historical or Chronological Approach. The historical or chronological approach is the easiest to follow and is suitable for job-seekers with limited experience. The chronological sequence, in inverse order, determines how items are to be listed. It allows you to emphasize your current activity as the most important, whether that activity is the status of your training to date or the imminent completion of your studies or military service assignment. The danger in this approach lies in the temptation to write simply a fact sheet without highlighting significant features. It is also a challenge to find an attractive typographical layout for this approach so that the dates will not dominate. Dates do not sell your ability.

Functional Approach. In this type of resume, experience and education are arranged in the order of their importance with the most significant first, regardless of chronological sequence. The job title or job function is featured to indicate the responsibility and authority involved. Although names of schools and employers are subordinated to job title or function, they are included in the description. Dates, if given, are inconspicuous.

Experienced workers often find a functional approach the most logical way to display their qualifications. Such an approach is primarily useful when you have impressive job titles or duties to feature. If you have limited experience but some of your part-time and temporary jobs were within your career field, you may successfully apply a functional approach to your resume.

Analytical Approach. Like the functional approach, the analytical approach ignores historical sequence; unlike the functional, the analytical approach stresses skills and abilities regardless of where they were developed and demonstrated.

This approach offers you a way of arranging your experience into significant groups of abilities and accomplishments which help to support your career goal. Names of employers and schools do not need to be tagged to each item as you may have exercised these skills in several positions.

An analytical approach is especially appropriate when the actual duties and skills developed in your school and work experience are more impressive than your job titles or length of experience. This approach, or an adaptation of it, is probably the best way to write a resume when you have recently shifted career goals or if your experiences have been primarily of a voluntary nature. You need to exploit your qualifications thoroughly to show how they support your new objective.

Informal or Imaginative Approach. An imaginative approach may be an adaptation of any of the other approaches or it may be entirely original. For example, you may emphasize your personal potentials giving illustrations from incidents where you displayed these qualities; or you may quote from testimonial letters written about you by teachers, former employers, or other professional contacts. You may even choose to use a medium other than print.

Newcomers to the employment market will find an informal or imaginative approach quite effective in calling attention to their potential as employees - providing good taste is evident. It is usually better to be too conservative than too flamboyant (unless you are applying for a job in the arts where a high premium is placed on such innovation). Applying for a job is a serious matter and employers expect you to be serious if you are sincere.

1627 South Street, DeKalb, Illinois 60115   (815)756-5365

Type of Work Desired: Would like to work closely with adolescents in either a community or institutional setting.

Volunteer Experience

Jefferson Elementary School, DeKalb, Illinois.
> Worked with learning disabled children in a Diagnostic/Resource area. Taught in individual and small group situations. Developed and implemented prescriptive remedial programs for several children (in reading, self-concept and verbal expression). January 1976 to April 1976.

DeKalb County Villages, DeKalb, Illinois.
> Became acquainted with the problem areas of youth including drug dependence, truancy, inability to accept authority and usually a negative self-concept. Worked with individuals on target behaviors and implemented the behavioral system. Designed a low cost activities list. Overall, maintained good relationships with both residents and staff. June 1975 and September 1975 to December 1975.

Illinois Youth Center, Geneva, Illinois.
> Tutored in mathematics and in GED program. Assisted in developing and carrying out evening activities. January 1975 to May 1975.

Youth Services Bureau, Drop in Center, DeKalb Illinois.
> Supervised and participated in on going activities (pool and ping pong). Functioned as a role model for the adolescents. February 1974 to May 1974.

Work Experience

Solo Cup Company, Highland Park, Illinois, May 1975 to August 1975 and December 1975 to January 1976.

Pickle Barrel Restaurant, Northbrook, Illinois, May 1974 to August 1974.

Children's Village, Sales Department, Highland Park, Illinois, September 1971 to August 1972 and June 1973 to August 1973.

Topps Discount Store, Domestics and Snack Bar, Highland Park, Illinois, August 1969 to July 1971.

Education

Bachelor of Arts Degree in Psychology at Northern Illinois University, May 1976 with cum laude distinction.

High School Diploma from Deerfield High School, Deerfield, Illinois, June 1972.

Activities

Undergraduate Psychological Association,
Alpha Delta Pi Sorority, Assistant Panhellenic Representative.
Phi Kappan Sigma Little Sister Organization, Corresponding Secretary.
Enjoy gymnastics, camping, cooking, plants, softball, and fine arts.

References

References will be made available upon request.

ARNOLD M. ARNST

915 Hillcrest
Apartment #13C
DeKalb, Illinois 60115
(815) 756-7000

Home Address: 454 North First Street
Westchester, Illinois 62354
(312) 459-1687

JOB OBJECTIVE: I am seeking an entry level accounting position with a company where I will best be able to apply my accounting knowledge and be presented with advancement opportunities once I have proven myself capable.

EDUCATION:

1975-
1976

Northern Illinois University
   Major: Accountancy
   Overall Accy. GPA: 2.96/4.0

Bachelor of Science
   Accountancy

Carthage College: Kenosha, WI
   Major: Business Administration

No Degree

I have earned an estimated 70% of my college expenses.

WORK
EXPERIENCE

Jan. 1977-
present

I am currently working 12-15 hours per week at Hardee's restaurant in DeKalb. Because of a demonstrated leadership ability, I have been left in charge of the store on numerous occasions and am capable of handling an eight hour shift without supervision.

Summers:
1976

While attending summer school at NIU, I worked 40 hours per week in the warehouse of Del Monte Corporation's can manufacturing plant in Rochelle, Illinois. Through the proper budgeting of my time, I was able to give maximum effort to and receive very rewarding results from both activities.

1975

I drove the "empty can" truck for one of Del Monte Corporation's canning factories in Rochelle. It was my responsibility to keep the plant supplied with cans so operation could be continually performed.

1973-
1974

I worked full-time my last two months of high school and the following summer for Illinois Yarn Company in Rochelle. Because of my worthy performance, I was able to work when home from college.

ACTIVITIES: Member, Beta Phi Epsilon Fraternity, Carthage College
                Member, Student Accounting Society, Northern Illinois University
                Participated in intramural sports in college

PERSONAL DATA: Birthdate: 8/24/55   Height: 6'3"
                Health: Excellent   Weight: 180

REFERENCES: Will be made available upon request.

Clorissa Crenshaw
4231 High Street
Elgin, IL   62351
312/543-8765

Marital Status: single

Date & Place of Birth: January 4, 1948, Chicago, Ill.

Age: 29

Health: excellent

Education:

Master's of Science, Counselor Education, Northern Illinois University, 1974.
Bachelor of Arts, English, Northern Illinois University, 1970.
Downers Grove High School, 1965.
Presently working toward a Certificate of Advanced Study in Counseling and
    Community Mental Health, Expected date of completion: December, 1977.

Occupational Experiences:

Counselor, Community Crisis Center, April, 1976 to the present.

The Community Crisis Center is a 24-hour shelter facility for women-in-crisis.
The Crisis Center serves persons in crises involving family or marital problems,
child neglect or abuse, alcohol and drug abuse and woman abuse. The counselor
at the Center has charge of all client programs and supervises the delivery
of all direct services. Her responsibilities include intake, case management,
daily counseling during their stay and continuing contact after they leave the
Center. She also supervises the four resident counselors, conducting daily
staffings and inservice training.

Graduate Research Assistant, Student Teaching Office, N.I.U. September, 1975
    to April, 1976.

Duties included examination and selection of artifacts for the History of
Education Collection.

Technical Assistant, Counseling Laboratory, N.I.U. Summer Session, 1975.

The technical assistant was responsible for the laboratory and its clinical
facilities.

Assistant Investigator, Project Discover. September, 1974 to September, 1975.

Project Discover is a computer-based vocational education and information system. Discover expands upon the C.V.I.S. model with a program which has been adapted for all age groups. The submodule designed during this project is a decision-making game with both junior high and high school versions. The game has been published both by IBM and the Psychological Corporation.

Graduate Teaching Assistant, Learning Center, N.I.U. September, 1973 to September, 1974.

Clerical Supervisor, Government Documents Department, N.I.U. Libraries. 1971 to 1973.

Library Technical Assistant, N.I.U. Libraries, 1970 to 1971.

Field Experience:

Doctoral level practicums in both group and individual counseling supervised through the counseling department.

Counselor and counseling supervisor, Women's Studies Center, N.I.U., 1974 to 1976.

The counselor at the Women's Studies Center served as counselor for any woman in the community requesting services. The counselor also designed and taught a course on peer counseling.

Other Pertinent Data:

I am currently completing work on a descriptive study of abused women which will include statistics from instruments measuring self-concept and locus of control as well as data obtained from questionnaires.

References are available upon request.

TERESA LYNN SMITH
86 South Belmont Ave. Arlington Heights, Illinois   60005

EDUCATION

Bachelor of Science: Journalism/Advertising
   (1977)
     Minor emphasis: Marketing
     Communication studies
Northern Illinois University - DeKalb, Illinois

PERSONAL DATA

Telephone: 312 - 259-7777
Height: 5'8"
Weight: 125 lbs.
Health: Excellent
Marital Status: Single

TRAINING

Advertising copywriting
Media planning
Developing comprehensive advertising and
   public relations campaigns
Writing and filming public service
   announcements for DeKalb area cable
   television
Writing and taping television storyboards
   and radio scripts
Layout and graphic processes experience

ACTIVITIES

Who's Who Among Student in
   American Colleges and
   Universities
Dean's list
Omicron Delta Kappan (na-
   tional leadership honorary)
Holmes Student Center Public
   Relations Committee
Cormitory Council Publicity
   Committee
National Orientation
   Director's Conference
Resident Assistant Appeals
   Board

EXPERIENCE

Selected to compete in American Advertising
   Federation national student competition
Supervisor, Holmes Student Center
Counselor, Department of Orientation, NIU
Resident Assistant, NIU
Central Desk Receptionist, NIU

REFERENCES

References and portfolio
   are available upon
   request.

ADVERTISING

Maria Magillicutti

ADDRESS

P.O. Box 333
DeKalb, Illinois 60115
Phone: (815) 758-2222

PERSONAL DATA

Social Security Number: 012-34-5678
Birthdate: August 14, 1955
Sex: Female
Marital Status: Single
Height: 5 feet, 4 inches
Weight: 112 pounds
Health: Excellent

TEACHING AREA

I have been prepared in Elementary Education, Educable Mentally Handicapped
Education, and Physically Handicapped Education. I feel I can be a competent
teacher for each group. My main area of concentration has been with Physically
Handicapped learners in academic, social, and vocational areas. Consequently,
my main preference in job seeking is with any age group of Physically Handicapped children.

TEACHING OBJECTIVE

To help my students develop necessary living skills by providing them
with appropriate opportunities to facilitate learning. I view each student
as a potential learner, and believe it is my responsibility to make certain
that the environment and methods are conducive to maximum development of individual potential. In order to do this, I must stay informed of educational
developments and exhaust every possible resource.

EDUCATIONAL RECORD

Northern Illinois University   DeKalb, Illinois   Spring, 1977
Bachelor of Science Degree received in Elementary Education, Educable Mentally
Handicapped Education, and Physically Handicapped Education.

TEACHING EXPERIENCES

Student Teaching   Clinton Rosette Middle School
                     DeKalb, Illinois   Spring, 1977
    At Clinton Rosette I was involved in the multi-age community which is an

open-space, open education environment. I co-operated with two teachers, assuming classes in the areas of mathematics and social studies to sixth, seventh and eighth grade students. I also directed several mini-groups in the school learning center. In addition, I helped coach the girls track team through the entire season.

Student Teaching   Myrtle E. Huff Elementary School
                  Elgin, Illinois   Spring, 1977
     I student taught in the orthopedically handicapped classroom at Huff School. The students ranged in age from 5-13, and varied greatly in both abilities and disabilities. I assumed full responsibility for the intermediate and pre-school students. In doing so, I co-operated my efforts with the occupational therapist, physical therapist, speech therapist, and other itinerant personnel.

Group Leader   Camp Maple Leaf
              DeKalb, Illinois   Summer, 1977
     Camp Maple Leaf is a Special Education day camp for Educable Mentally Handicapped children. I will be a group leader, responsible for planning activities for an assigned group of campers.

VOLUNTEER COMMUNITY SERVICES

Big Sister Organization: DeKalb County Family Services 1976-Present
Hostess to Jacksonville School for the Blind: North Central Association of
   Schools for the Blind Annual Track Meet, DeKalb 1976
Physical Fitness Counselor: Sts. Peter & Paul, Chicago   1971-73

PROFESSIONAL ORGANIZATIONS

Member: Council for Exceptional Children 1973-Present
         Division of Physically Handicapped and Homebound
Member: Sigma Sigma Sigma Sorority 1974-Present
Member: Illinois Teachers of the Physically Handicapped

EMPLOYMENT HISTORY

Craft Supervisor Office of Campus Recreation 10/76 - 5/77
                  Northern Illinois University DeKalb, Illinois
Clerk and Cashier So-Fro Fabrics 12/75 - 5/77
                  2500 Sycamore Road DeKalb, Illinois
Hostess and Waitress Howard Johnson's, Inc. 7/75 - 11/76
                  Crego Road DeKalb, Illinois
Researcher and Typist Political Science Department 3/75 - 8/75
                  Northern Illinois University
                  DeKalb, Illinois
Cashier Ponderose Steak House 10/74 - 2/75
         1530 Sycamore Road DeKalb, Illinois

<u>Clerk and Typist</u> Blue Cross & Blue Shield Summer, 1974
                230 North Michigan Avenue   Chicago, Illinois
<u>Usherette</u> Andy Frain, Inc. Summers, 1972-73
                25 West Chicago Avenue   Chicago, Illinois

The above jobs help me finance 95% of my college expenses.

REFERENCES

References will be made available upon request. Credentials are on file at
the following address: CAREER PLANNING AND PLACEMENT CENTER
                             Northern Illinois University
                             Lowden Hall, Room 204
                             DeKalb, Illinois   60115
                             (815) 753-1641

HERMEINE HORSEMAN
3624 Grapevine Boulevard
Tarzana, California   94633
213/344-4395 or 213/346-5329

EXPERIENCE

RADIO: Wrote and edited news copy. Anchored and produced 5, 10, 15 and
30 minute newcasts. Directed 5 minute network/30 and 60 minute local
newscasts. Dubbed audio news inserts. Planned, directed, and coordinated day-to-day functioning of news staff. Programmed for FM and FM
computerized stations. Wrote, produced, and directed programming specials for AM and FM stations. Created promotion packages, produced
related spots, and initiated public contact. Supervised live variety
show. Managed major league baseball network, produced spots, and
directed broadcasts.

TELEVISION: Interviewed people for on-camera news inserts and magazine
pieces. Anchored and produced 15 minute newscast. Wrote and produced
a 30 minute documentary. Announced live, nighttime variety show, station
breaks and promotions. Read and evaluated incoming scripts for potential
use as series material. Wrote and distributed publicity releases for all
new and on-going series. Involved in casting for series and specials.

EMPLOYERS

Arthur Productions, Beverly Hills, California	1976-Present
Artemis Productions, Beverly Hills, California	1975
American Broadcasting Co., Centry City, California	1974
Warner Bros., Inc., Burbank, California	1972-1974
NBC-WMAQ, Chicago, Illinois	1969-1971
WSIU-FM, Carbondale, Illinois	1968

EDUCATION

Major: Radio/Television
Minor: English
Southern Illinois University, Carbondale, Illinois
Bachelor of Science 1969

PERSONAL

Date of Birth: December 12, 1945
Status: Single

REFERENCES

Available on request

```
****************************************************************
DEBRA A. DELUX              23 Hillcrest Apt. 543
15609 Avalon Avenue         DeKalb, IL  60115 (School)
South Holland, IL  60474 (Home)  815-758-111
****************************************************************
```

CAREER GOAL: PROFESSIONAL PUBLIC RELATIONS REPRESENTATIVE. Desire position
               where use can be made of communication skills, research, analysis
               and evaluation skills in promoting the active support of an or-
               ganization's various publics.

EDUCATION: Thornton Community College 1972-1974 A.A. Degree
               South Holland, IL

               Northern Illinois University 1975 -   Major: B.S. Journalism
               DeKalb, IL   May 1977 Minor: Political Science

               Public Relations Emphasis

               Journalistic Writing   Industrial Press Writing
               Principles of Public Relations Copy Editing and Rewrite
               Advanced Public Relations   Press Photography
               Article Writing   Principles of Marketing
               Graphics of Communication   Public Administration

EXPERIENCE: Public Relations Intern, Burson-Martsteller Public Relations/
               Public Affairs, Chicago, IL. Part-time during senior year.
               1976-1977. Completed many diverse assignments for a variety
               of clients while participating in NIU Professional-Amateur
               (PRO-AM) Program.

               Fashion Coordinator, Sears, Roebuck & Co., Calumet City, IL.
               1971-72. As member of Sears Fashion Board, Coordinated weekly
               fashion shows and also modeled in shows.

               Teller, First National Bank of Dolton, IL. 1973-1977. Part-
               time while attending college. Earned half of total expenses.

ACTIVITIES: Member of NIU PRSSA Chapter, helped produce chapter newsletter.
               Reporter and columnist for Thornton College newspaper.
               Member of Thornton College Student Government.

PERSONAL   Health: Excellent   Birthdate: 3-25-55
DATA
               Available in May

               References on request.

93

JORDAN BORDEN
023 S. Pine
Waterman, IL 60556
Telephone: 815-264-4444

Age: 36 Married
Health: Excellent
Available: June

VOCATIONAL GOAL: A career with no limits on my potential or compensation.
 An opportunity which offers challenges and also lets me increase my responsibilities and utilize my skills of organizing and coordination, analyzing
 problems and decision making, sales and self-motivation, and dealing with
 people.

BACKGROUND: BS in Education with emphasis in math and language arts. Eighteen hours of coursework in Business Administration with emphasis on accounting, data processing, and business law. Taught elementary school in Waterman,
 IL for eleven years. Managed own real estate office. Set up and directed
 summer math program. Participated in and helped compile results of a pilot
 study in behavior modification.

AREAS OF SKILLS AND ABILITIES

ORGANIZING AND COORDINATION: As a Teacher I planned lessons which provided
 for individual differences in a classroom of about twenty-three students.
 As a Supervisor of student teachers the responsibilities included supervision
 and instruction in methods, media, techniques, and subject materials. As
 the Director of the summer math program I was responsible for selecting,
 ordering material, and writing proposals to obtain federal funding.

SELF-MOTIVATION AND SALES: An example of my self-motivation was my desire
 to obtain my real estate brokers license. I studied on my own and after
 passing my exam established my own business on a part-time basis. As a Real
 Estate Broker I secured listings, showed property, prepared closing statements and offers of purchase, and helped obtain financing. It was also my
 responsibility to prepare advertisements and negotiate sales. In addition,
 I have a good foundation of basic business understanding.

ANALYZING PROBLEMS AND DECISION MAKING: I demonstrated my competence in
 analyzing problems through identifying strengths and weaknesses of students
 I taught. I decided how to deal with each situation in the most effective
 manner. While working on the behavior modification pilot study, I made
 decisions as to the effectiveness of the results of the program. I am
 constantly making decisions which have a lasting effect in my teaching.

DEALING WITH PEOPLE: As a teacher and real estate broker I enjoy dealing with
 people and believe that I am effective in doing this. I am an active member
 in church and community activities and have been selected for positions of
 responsibility which require a proficiency in dealing with people of all ages.

REFERENCES: Will be furnished upon request.

94

Cover Letter Are Where It's At -- For every resume you sent out, you will need a cover letter to accompany it. The major function of a cover letter is to create enough interest in you to make the employer go on to read your resume. Give the reader some idea that you are a person who is different, who does not deal with stereotypes. Remember that you are selling yourself, that this letter is part of your marketing campaign. If your letter is not prepared with that in mind, then your resume will probably never be read.

The letter should be concise. It should also be short. You should be able to tell your story in 200 to 250 words. Don't get involved in long explanations - what you want is an interview. You can go into details there.

Get some knowledge of the business or school to which you are writing. If you think that it is a conservative organization, then don't write a "flashy" letter. If you are seeking out a position in a laboratory or in design or research, then don't write a hard sell letter. This kind of letter is best used with the organization where you want to be a salesperson.

A cover letter should cover four basic areas. It should <u>picture</u> what you have to offer the employer.

<u>EXAMPLE</u>

In your advertisement in the April 14 edition of the <u>Chicago Tribune</u> you asked for a major in biology with considerable emphasis in chemistry for a technician's position in your laboratory. Wouldn't you really rather have a biochemist?

Your cover letter should also <u>promise</u> and <u>prove</u> you can do the type of job you are applying for by making reference to personal traits and previously demonstrated experience.

EXAMPLE

My baccalaureate degree work at Northern Illinois University has included class work in immunology, microbiology, radio-isotope techniques, and biological chemistry. Through regularly assigned laboratory work I have learned to use the mass spectrometer, gas chromotography, and column chromotography equipment. I utilized photo spectrometry equipment in an independent research project involving radio-isotopes.

The enclosed resume will give additional details of my work and education background. I would like to call your attention to the two summers that I spent working in the laboratories at Michael Reese Hospital, however, where I acquired a thorough understanding of laboratory procedures.

Finally, you should push for an interview. This last point can be presented in a variety of ways and is basically whatever you feel comfortable with.

EXAMPLES

I'll be in town next Friday around 2:00 p.m. and will stop by to see you then...

I'd like to talk with you about any position you might have available in my area; I'll be calling you within the week to see if there is a mutual time we can get together...

I can be available for an interview any time at your convenience...

You may develop one basic letter that can be changed slightly for the different places you are going to send it. However, it is essential that you type each letter individually, and make each one a little different from the other. Mass produced letters are not recommended.

Though your letter should follow the regular business format, try to make your letter as personal as possible. Try to identify a specific individual who will be in a position to say "you're hired" and direct your correspondence to him or her. If you are following up with a phone call, it will be this specific person you will be calling.

96

Cover letters can be used to inquire about possible job openings in your field, or to apply for actual known vacancies. In addition, it is often advisable to send a thank-you letter in follow-up to an interview with an employer. An example of each of these types of letters follows.

1308 Westmont Avenue
Dolton, Illinois 60474
August 24, 1977

Mr. David L. Ruggles, Senior Partner
Ruggles, Smith and Jones
111 West Monroe Street
Chicago, Illinois 60603

Dear Mr. Ruggles:

Will there be a need in your firm for a young Management Trainee who will offer you a sound educational background (MBA degree in June, 1978) and a willingness to work hard?

My objective is not just a position of responsibility, but the opportunity for job satisfaction of utilizing my abilities and educational training to the fullest extent. Finance and Accounting are areas where I might best contribute to your firm, because of my strong interest in these fields.

May I come in and chat with you or another executive of your firm? If there is a need where you think I might fit, I believe I can assure you of my value. My resume is enclosed, and provides a more detailed description of my qualifications. I'll be available in May, 1978, upon graduation.

I look forward to your reply.

Very truly yours,

Oscar M. Ogles

Enc.

DRUSCILLA DRYSDALE
1416 Briar Place
Chicago, Illinois   60657
Telephone: (312) 488-6806

August 24, 1977

Mr. John Jones, Advertising Director
ABC Company
1612 W. Farwell
Chicago, Illinois   60626

Dear Mr. Jones:

Would your company benefit from the services of a creative, innovative writer
...if my work resulted in sales, profits, and a better company reputation in
the community? I think I can make that kind of a contribution.

I've used my excellent journalism background to some degree in my work as a
teacher. Now I seek a full-time opportunity to pursue my chosen field as a
career.

My experience, training and strong desire for this field of work qualify me
to successfully handle such a position. My resume is enclosed.

Will you be willing to let me come in to chat with you for a few minutes?

Very truly yours,

Druscilla Drysdale

Enc.

823 Student Drive
DeKalb, Illinois   60115
August 26, 1977

Mr. C.D. Roe
Superintendent of Schools
Community Unit S/D 314
Central City, Illinois   62801

Dear Mr. Roe:

Your fifth grade vacancy interests me greatly. My four years of preparation
at Northern Illinois University have been in elementary education; I am particularly interested in the ten to twelve-year old age group.

A week's supervision of elementary students at Lorado Taft Field Campus served
as an especially valuable experience in preparation for this work. My student
teaching was done in the fifth grade at the University School on the campus.
As a member of the college band and the newspaper staff I learned the importance
of coordinated work which, I am sure, will be helpful in working with fifth
graders.

My qualifications are presented in the enclosed data sheet, and the Career
Planning and Placement Center at NIU will forward my complete credentials at
your request.

I am looking forward to visiting Central City for an interview. The next three
weekends are open to me, but I shall be glad to come at any time convenient
for you. I will call you on Thursday, September 1, to set a definite interview
date.

Sincerely,

Lucy Picardo

Enclosure

236 Larkspur Lane
Happyville, IL   61234
August 22, 1977

Mr. M. Ployer
XYZ Corporation of America
XYZ Plaza
Chicago, IL   60606

Dear Mr. Ployer:

I wish to thank you for the courtesy you extended to me during our interview
yesterday. Your answers to my questions served to confirm my interest in
employment with the XYZ Corporation of America.

I feel that I have a genuine contribution to make to your firm and I look
forward to discussing this with you in the future. Please contact me if you
should need further information.

Once again, thank you.

                        Sincerely,

                        Nancy Drew

NORTHERN ILLINOIS UNIVERSITY
DeKalb, Illinois   60115

Office of the Career Planning and
Placement Center

815   753   1641
815   753   1643

WELCOME TO OUR OFFICE

The purpose of this communication is to explain and provide information
about establishing, utilizing, and maintaining your credential file. Our
office serves as a repository for the safe, efficient housing and maintenance
of your credentials. To enable us to better serve you, please take care in
reading and complying with the following instructions - Thank you.

Credential Staff

WHO MAY ESTABLISH CREDENTIALS

* Any persons who have earned their highest degree (i.e. bachelor's, master's,
Certificate of Advanced Study, or doctorate) from NIU, or one who has earned
certification and has not established a credential elsewhere.
* Graduate students who are in a degree program and will have earned a total
of at least 15 hours at NIU in the semester in which they register for services.
* Undergraduates in their senior year who request the services.

CATEGORIES OF SERVICE

Full alumni Services (fee $15 annually) allows candidate to:
  1.) Establish, reactivate, or comprehensively update credential file.
  2.) Request referral services.
  3.) Send seven sets of credentials to prospective employers at no charge,
       and additional sets at the rate of $2 per set.
  4.) Utilize CPPC counseling services, on-campus interviews, workshops,
       resource library, and vacancy listings on view in our office.
  5.) Receive Education vacancies for three months. Additional subscrip-
       tions are available for $3 for three months.

Current Student Services (no fee) allows candidate to:
  1.) Establish, reactivate, or update credential file.
  2.) Request referral services.
  3.) Send seven sets of credentials to prospective employers at no charge
       and additional sets at the rate of $1 per set.
  4.) Utilize CPPC counseling services, on-campus interviews, workshops,
       resource library, and vacancy listings on view in our office.

5.) Subscribe to <u>Education vacancies</u> for $3 for three months.

<u>Limited Alumni Services</u> (Fees as indicated) allows candidate to:
1.) Comprehensively update or reactivate credential file ($2).
2.) Send credentials to prospective employers ($2 for each set).
3.) Utilize CPPC counseling services, on-campus interviews, workshops, resource library, and vacancy listings on view in our office.
4.) Subscribe to <u>Education vacancies</u> for $3 for three months.
5.) Register for Full Alumni Services at any time for an annual fee of $15.

<u>Inactive Status Services</u> (no fee) allows candidate to:
1.) Establish credentials.
2.) Make minor revisions (name, address changes) on original form.
3.) Add letters of reference.
4.) Activate credentials at any time.

REGISTRATION MATERIALS AND INSTRUCTIONS

<u>Registration Form</u>:
1.) Complete the information section beginning with your last name. Do not leave any areas blank.
2.) Indicate the type of service you are registering for by checking the category which applies to you (see CATEGORIES OF SERVICE on front page).
3.) Check the appropriate blank(s) which indicates your fee schedule and, where applicable, indicate what month you would like your subscription to <u>Education vacancies</u> to begin.

<u>Data Cover Sheet</u>

Exercise care in completing your Data Cover Sheet. This form is reproduced and sent to prospective employers exactly as you submit it. Information should be typed or printed neatly using black ink.

1.) Personal Information. This is self-explanatory. Always keep us informed of your name, current address, phone, and/or changes.
2.) Educational Record. Provide information in reverse chronological order. Listing only those colleges or universities where degrees have been earned or where a significant amount of course work has been taken.
3.) Teaching Certificate. Check all levels or areas in which you are certified or certifiable upon completion of current college work.
4.) Student Teaching. Provide information as indicated.
5.) Extra-curricular Activity. There are no specific certification requirements for extra-curricular assignments. You must however, be able to demonstrate a certain level of competency or skill depending on the assignment.

6.) Significant Employment Experience. List last employer first.
Volunteer experience may be used. Student Teaching may be used if
you have no other experience to list.

7.) Type of Employment Preferred. This refers to the kind of position
desired, such as classroom teacher, counselor, principal, superintendent, professor, dean, and so forth, as well as the level, or the
type of institution.

8.) Location Preference. Indicate geographic preferences or restrictions
you may have. Terms such as Illinois, Midwest, Open, Mobile, 30
mile radius of Chicago, may be used.

9.) Date of availability. Give date when you would be able to start
work.

Record of Courses (Optional)

The CP&PC is not permitted to include an official transcript in your file;
however, in many instances, information provided about course work may suffice
for hiring purposes. Undergraduates should list courses in their major, minor,
and/or courses related to the type of employment sought. All graduate course
work should be included.

Authorization and Agreement Form

If a completed Authorization Form does not appear in your file, your credentials cannot, under law, be released to prospective employers. This form must
be completed before a file can be officially established.

Personal Reference Forms

Accurately type all information requested in the top section. Consider carefully each option with regard to the right of access to the reference. Each
option has both advantages and disadvantages. Do not have references submitted
to our office until you have filed your forms with us.

Reference Card

Indicate on this card the names of persons you have requested to write references on your behalf.

Referral Information Card

Type or print with pen. Do not bend or fold. The numbers below pertain to
specific sections of the Referral Information Card.

1.) Do not mark in shaded areas. (Shaded area for Office Use Only.)
2.) Provide personal data, including previous surname if applicable.
3.) The blanks for hours are those in your major/minor or area of

emphasis. List subject areas in which you have earned 15 or more
hours.

4.) Subjects/grades should be listed in order of preference.
5.) Indicate Preferences.
6.) Teaching experience may include permanent assignments or related
volunteer work.
7.) Indicate date you will be able to start work and the date you submit
this form.
8.) Indicate grade point average in your major area and the date of your
highest degree.
9.) Indicate which option you marked on the Authorization Form.
10.) Circle the terms that best describe your current status and preferences. Identify additional items not listed by completing spaces
marked "other".
11.) Same as Number 10.

Any active candidate is entitled to be referred, when appropriate, to prospective employers. To be eligible for referral service, the following steps must
be taken:

1.) Complete the Referral Information Card. This automatically activates
your file for referrals for the quarter of the year during which it
is submitted. If request is submitted during last half of the quarter,
you will remain active during the next quarter.
2.) If you want to continue to be referred during the next quarter, you
must notify CP&PC sometime during the last half of the current
quarter. This may be done by submitting one of the enclosed Referral
Update Cards, or by letter. You may request to be on active referral
for one quarter at a time.
3.) Upon accepting employment, notify CP&PC by sending in Referral Update
Card or a letter with appropriate information.

Referral Update Cards

This packet includes three Referral Update Cards for you to use to notify us
of your referral status. This may also be done by letter. Please notify CP&PC
when you have accepted employment.

REQUESTING CREDENTIALS

Requests to send credentials to prospective employers are to be made in writing,
preferably using the enclosed Request for Credentials Form. List the name of
the school or business where your credentials are to be mailed, the date you are
making the credential request, your name, telephoning number and social security
number. Provide the name and title of the employer, name of school or business,
street address, city, state and zip code, where appropriate. Credentials should
not be confused with transcripts. CP&PC is not permitted to reproduce official

transcripts; this is the responsibility of the Office of Registration and Records, Altgeld Hall, Room 212, Northern Illinois University, DeKalb, IL 60115. Telephone: 815/753-0680.

RIGHTS OF REGISTRANTS

Open or Closed Credential File

It is the right of registrants to determine if certain information is to be classified open (accessible to them) or closed (confidential).

Personal Copies of Credentials

Registrants and non-registrants may request a copy of their credential for personal use. The copy will be stamped "For Personal Use Only" and is not intended to be used for employment purposes. Closed letters, or letters written prior to November 19, 1974, will not be included in the personal copy. Requests for personal copies of the file must be made in writing and will be treated as a regular credential request.

Viewing of Credentials

Current students and alumni may view their open credentials by request and by following the instructions found on the bulletin board in the entrance to CP&PC.

RETURN ALL COMPLETED FORMS TO CP&PC

OFFICE HOURS
8:00 am to 5:00 pm
Monday thru Friday

Northern Illinois University ⬛
DeKalb, Illinois 60115

The Career Planning
and Placement Center
210 Swen Parson Hall — North
815 753 1641

MEMORANDUM

SUBJECT: New Forms for Credential Services

TO: Northern Illinois Students and Alumni

FROM: Career Planning and Placement Center

This packet contains forms that must be completed and returned to our office for the initiation or maintenance of a credential file.

Please read all instructions and complete forms with care. Be sure to return the "Registration for Placement Services Form," and check the type of services desired. If fees have been indicated for these services, please enclose a check for the proper amount, made payable to Northern Illinois University.

IMPORTANT: You are eligible for "Current Student Services" with regard to credentials if:

(1)   You are a full or part-time degree candidate in your final year before graduation.

(2)   You have received a degree from NIU within the past year.

CAREER PLANNING AND PLACEMENT CENTER
NORTHERN ILLINOIS UNIVERSITY
DeKalb, Illinois 60115
815 / 753-1641

REGISTRATION FOR
PLACEMENT CREDENTIAL SERVICES

NAME _____
      Last   First   Middle   Former Surname

Mailing Address _____
         Street   City   State   Zip Code

Most Recent Graduation _____ Degree and Major _____
             Month   Year

No. of EARNED Graduate Hours: _____ No. Semester Hours Currently Enrolled _____

If in a degree program, please indicate proposed date of graduation. _____

Do you currently have a Credential File at NIU Placement Office?   Yes ☐   No ☐

****

PLEASE CHECK SERVICE DESIRED

☐Full Alumni   ☐Current Student   ☐Limited Alumni   ☐Inactive

FEES

_____ $15.00   Full Alumni Services

_____ 3.00   Education Vacancies, weekly for 3 months. Beginning Month _____

_____ 2.00   Comprehensive Credential File Updating

_____ 2.00   Credential File Mailed to Prospective Employer, for EACH REQUEST

_____ Total Amount Remitted with Registration

Date _____

DATA COVER SHEET

PERSONAL INFORMATION

Office of the Career Planning
and Placement Center
Lowden Hall 204
815 753 1641
815 753 1643

Name _____
     First   Middle   Last

Current
Address _____ Until_____ Phone (_____)_____
     Number and Street   City   State   Zip

Permanent
Address _____ Phone (_____)_____
     Number and Street   City   State   Zip

Social Security Number_____ – _____ – _____ U.S. Citizen_____ If not, Type of Visa _____

Date of Last Graduation _____ Current Date _____

EDUCATIONAL RECORD (Most recent degrees or dates of attendance first)

Names of Colleges or Universities and Location	Dates Attended	Major Area of Study	No. of Credits	Areas of Emphasis with 15 or more Credit Hours	No. of Credits	Degree Month/Year

TEACHING CERTIFICATE—if applicable

Elementary _____   Vocational _____   Administration _____

Secondary _____   Special Education _____   Other (Specify) _____

STUDENT TEACHING
Location   Date   Level

_____ _____ Preschool _____ Elementary _____ Jr. H.S. or Middle School _____ H.S. _____

_____ _____ Preschool _____ Elementary _____ Jr. H.S. or Middle School _____ H.S. _____

EXTRACURRICULAR ACTIVITIES—which you feel competent to handle:

_____ _____ _____ _____
_____ _____ _____ _____

SIGNIFICANT EMPLOYMENT EXPERIENCE (Please list last employer first)

Dates Employed	Name of Employer & Address	Your Position or Responsibilities

Type of Employment Preferred _____

Locational Preferences _____ Date of Availability _____

RECORD OF COURSES

_____
Candidate

Related Undergraduate Courses						All Graduate Courses				
Title of Course	Course Number	Year	Semester Hours	Grade		Title of Course	Course Number	Year	Semester Hours	Grade

Note: This form was filled out by the applicant and Career Planning & Placement assumes no responsibility for the accuracy of its contents.

CAREER PLANNING AND PLACEMENT CENTER
NORTHERN ILLINOIS UNIVERSITY
DeKalb, Illinois   60115
815/753-1641

AUTHORIZATION AND AGREEMENT FORM

(1) Pursuant to the "Family Educational Rights and Privacy Act of 1974," as amended, and the Regulations promulgated thereunder, I authorize the Career Planning and Placement Center of Northern Illinois University to collect and maintain a file of credentials for the purpose of assisting me in my search for employment.

(2) I further authorize the Career Planning and Placement Center to send my credentials to prospective employers under the following guidelines:

_____1.   Only as requested by me.

_____2.   As requested by me or at the request of a prospective employer.

_____3.   As requested by me, or a prospective employer, or professional staff member of the Career Planning and Placement Center.

(Optional) - In addition to the person or persons identified above, I authorize:

_____/_____

Name   Relationship

to request the mailing of my credential to a potential employer.

I understand that information received by the Career Planning and Placement Center will be open to me with the following exceptions:

(1)   Confidential references dated prior to November 19, 1974
(2)   References to which I have waived the right of access.

I am aware that, as a registrant, ALL policies and procedures of the Career Planning and Placement Center apply to me regarding completion of forms, payment of appropriate fees, and the use of my credentials.

Date_____   NAME_____
                                    Please Print
                                Signature_____

TO BE COMPLETED BY CANDIDATE BEFORE SUBMITTING TO WRITER: (Please Type)

Candidate's Name _____

| Last | First | Middle |

"I authorize _____ *to write a reference which will become a part*
of my credential on file with the Career Planning and Placement Center, NIU."

I voluntarily waive my right of access to this
recommendation under Public Law 93-380 and
the Regulations promulgated thereunder so that
it may be kept confidential.

If this waiver has not been signed, Public Law
93-380 and the Regulations promulgated
thereunder permits the inspection of this
recommendation by the candidate.

_____
Signature of Applicant

EVALUATION OF CANDIDATE

If you wish to support your written evaluation by completing the following checklist, do so using the following scale: *1 Superior; 2 Very Good;*
3 Good; 4 Fair; 5 Poor. If in doubt, leave space blank.

	1	2	3	4	5			1	2	3	4	5
Personality							Poise and Self-confidence					
Knowledge of Subject							Dependability					
Professional Attitude							Cooperation					
Organizing and Planning							Ability to Communicate					
Initiative							Adaptability					
Leadership							Creativity					

Submitted by:
Signature of Reference _____ Date _____

Position _____ Business Phone _____

Business Address _____

City / State / Zip Code _____

This is a form card (FORM K55-8118-55).

ADMINISTRATION
- Adm. Cent. Off.
- Adm. Elem.
- Adm. Sec.
- Adm. Coll.

ART

BUS. ED.
- Typing
- Shorthand
- Accountancy
- Business Law

COUNS. & GUID.

EARLY CHILD.

EARLY ELEM.

LATER ELEM.

ENGLISH
- Journalism
- Reading

FOREIGN LANG.
- French
- Spanish

HOME ECON.

IND. & TECH.
- Woods
- Draft
- Auto
- Metals

LIBRARY SCI.
- Inst. Media

MATH

MUSIC
- Instrumental
- Vocal

PHYSICAL ED.
- Health
- Driver Educ.

SCIENCE
- Biology
- Chemistry
- Physical

SOCIAL STUDIES
- History
- Economics
- Government
- Political Sci.

SPEECH
- Theatre

SPECIAL EDUC.
- EMH/THM
- LD/ED
- Phys. Handi.
- Vis. — Hear.
- Speech Ther.

① SHADED AREA FOR OFFICE USE ONLY
REFERRAL INFORMATION CARD

② Name: Last ___ First ___ Middle ___ (Former Surname)
Permanent Address ___ Street ___ City ___ State ___ Zip
Current Address ___ Street ___ City ___ State ___ Zip
Campus Phone ___ (Area Code)
Permanent Phone ___ (Area Code)

③ Major (Undergraduate) ___ Minor(s) ___ Hrs. ___ or ___ Hrs.
④ Major (Graduate) ___ Emphasis ___ Hrs. ___ Hrs.
⑤ List subjects/grades you prefer to teach; or other position or employment.
1. 2. 3. 4.

Do you desire a position that includes coaching? Yes ☐ No ☐
Are you willing to relocate? Yes ☐ No ☐
⑥ If (No), how far are you willing to commute? ___ Miles
⑦ Teaching Experience (Subject/Grade Level) ___ School ___ Dates From ___ To ___ / From ___ To ___ / From ___ To ___

Date Available: ___ Current Date: ___

⑧ G.P.A.
- 2.0–2.4
- 2.5–2.9
- 3.0–3.4
- 3.5–4.0
Major ___

DATE OF HIGHEST DEGREE
Month ___ Year ___

⑨ CREDENTIAL OPTION
1. 2. 3.

⑩ Circle terms that best describe your current status.

CERTIFICATE
- Std. Sec. 6-12
- Std. El. K-8
- Std. Spec. K-12
- Sp. Ed. Elem.
- Sp. Ed. Sec.
- LD/ED
- Adm. Ctf.
- Super. Endor.
- Other

TEACH. PREF.
- Pre School
- Elementary
- JH/Middle
- Sr. HS
- Counseling
- El. Adm.
- Sec. Adm.
- Central Off.
- Comm. Coll.
- Coll./Univ.

DEGREE
- Ed.D.
- C.A.S.
- M.S.
- B.S.

GEOGRAPHIC PREF.
- DeKalb Area
- City Chicago
- Chicago Sub.
- North. III.
- Illinois
- Mid-west
- Open
- Restrict./Other
- Other

⑪ Circle any of the extra curricular activities you feel competent to handle.
- Baseball
- Basketball
- Band
- Chorus
- Dance
- Debate
- Dramatics
- Field Hockey
- Football
- Golf
- Gymnast
- Hockey
- Plays
- Clubs
- Publication
- Soccer
- Swimming
- Tennis
- Track
- Volleyball
- Wrestling
- Other

FORM K55-8118-55

REFERRAL UP-DATE

Name_____ Phone_____ Date _____

Address _____

Major_____Degree _____ Date of Graduation _____

Please continue to keep my file active for referrals
for the following quarter (ONE QUARTER ONLY).

☐ Jan., Feb., Mar. ☐ Apr., May, June ☐ July, Aug., Sept. ☐ Oct., Nov., Dec.

Please discontinue referrals. Accepted Employment ☐

Other reason _____

Employed By _____ Position _____

Location _____ Salary (Annual) _____

Comments _____

_____

_____

_____

_____

Signature _____

REQUEST FOR CREDENTIALS

_____   _____
Your Name   Current Date

_____   _____
Telephone Number   Social Security Number

_____
Name and location of Organization where credentials are to be mailed.

_____

_____
Name and Title of hiring official

_____
Name of School or Business where credentials are to be mailed.

_____
Street Address

_____
City, State, and Zip Code

REFERENCE CARD
(Be sure to give all names in full)

SOCIAL SECURITY NO._____

NAME _____ Date _____
      Last   First   Middle

PRESENT ADDRESS   Date of Degree
                                   _____
_____   Major
                                   _____

List all references to be received:

Name	Professional Relationship to You	(DO NOT WRITE IN SPACE BELOW)

* Career Planning and Placement Center pocket, Northern Illinois University,
  DeKalb, 1980.

CHAPTER 5

MAJOR PROBLEMS IN TEACHING

The Teaching Profession

Most perceive that teaching is basically an applied science; that good teachers are trained by learning the scientific principles of human development, learning, evaluation and the like. Few teacher education programs seem to view teaching as an art. If schools of education viewed the "art" of teaching on a level equal to the "science" of instruction, one would find fewer nontenured, low ranking, part time faculty teaching the methods courses and supervising student teachers.

Those who teach in the elementary and secondary schools of our country are called teachers. On the other hand, those who teach in our colleges and universities almost always prefer to be called professors. Sometimes it has been assumed that teachers and professors are professional allies. In spite of the effort of many professional organizations to persuade the public that teaching is a profession, just as medicine and law are professions, one cannot help asking how teachers and professors view themselves and their work.

Those who teach in colleges and universities only rarely regard themselves as primary teachers, or formally ally themselves with teacher causes. Somehow the word 'professor' seems to have more status, as though a professor "professes" rather than teaches. One even finds college faculty members who hold the rank of instructor calling themselves college professors, so that the distinction

114

is not simply one of rank, but of institutional and social status. In fact teachers receive their training from the professors who in turn, very frequently exclude them as professional colleagues. By and large the college professor has had more years of training than the secondary or elementary teacher. He may enjoy greater respect within the community. Probably the most important distinction is the difference in duties expected of the college professor as opposed to the school teacher.

If teachers suffer from a diminished sense of self-worth and dignity, we might well look to the education profession itself - to the manner in which it honors and recognizes it's leaders, to the schools of education that prepare classroom teachers, to the role the classroom teachers play in the school.

The teacher is the central force that shapes the behaviors of the individual child as well as those of children in groups. The teacher is expected to possess a sufficient knowledge base of what is to be taught. However, many educators would question "source of information" as an appropriate role for teachers in a world where knowledge changes its form and substance at so rapid a pace. Although teaching may take many forms, the basic form is, of course, Instruction. This aspect of teaching includes three generic roles (1) planning for learning and instruction (2) facilitation of learning and instruction (3) evaluation of learning and instruction. The manner in which these roles are performed will vary from teacher to teacher. This is as it should be, because teacher's styles vary considerably. But essentially, each role makes basic provisions that enhance learning.

The teaching profession is a combination of variables. First is the image of the student; second is the professions' position relative to it; third is

the teacher's perception and fourth is the community's expectations. The

teacher must analyze each situation carefully, weighing the effects of each

variable on the situation. Only then can the role be performed in a manner

that will minimize counter-productive reactions.

Public Relations and the Teacher

Schools must be able to rally support for teachers, maintenance, and

equipment as well as buildings. Very often the public relations program is

neglected.

The key to public relations is "communications." Four groups are concerned.

These are the students, the teachers, the parents, and the community. It is

important that no double-talk be used or professional jargon or complicated

terms because public relations must be beamed at the total audience. We can

explain things in the laymen's language and we must have continuous effort in

the schools to bring about harmonious adjustment between the schools and its

public.

The objectives of public relations program should be: 1) to inform the

public about the work of the school, 2) to develop an awareness of the impor-

tance of the total education program, 3) to gain support for the school's

programs, 4) to acquaint the community with new educational trends and the

interpretation and use of these trends, 5) to improve the partnership concept

by uniting parents and teachers working together for the benefit of the

individual child, 6) to build the confidence of the school and to gain finan-

cial support for the total program, 7) to provide another avenue to interpret the school to the community and build good will for the school, 8) to upgrade

the entire educational program and to provide information to the children and

to the public of the various career opportunities that are available.

The administration working with the school faculty, the parent committees,

and with the involvement of students should make a thorough investigation of

the present public relations program to see if it meets the needs of that

individual district. Too often public relations is just "stuck in" and the

total program is never re-evaluated for the needs of the students. There must

be evidence to support the public relations program.

After carefully re-evaluating we should be able to rework and upgrade the

public relations program. Attention must be given to the entire community with

emphasis placed on individual students and their parents, the staff of the

individual school, the board of education, the influential groups in the com-

munity (Junior Chamber of Commerce, Lions Club, Kiwanas Club, Parent Teachers

Association) and so forth as well as the general public who support the schools

with their ever increasing tax dollar.

To be effective in public relations, the school must develop a workable

"sales pitch." This should be geared to the BENEFIT of the entire community

and both present and future children. It must stress the need for a better

understanding of the development of the individual student potential. It must

be built in positive terms with emphasis placed on the tremendous need to

adopt a systematic, well-planned purposeful public relations program.

The timing of any program is most important and must be handled carefully.

A general announcement can be made in the newspaper or mailed to the parents or put on the radio or on television. The announcement should state the objectives of the public relations program, the cost of the program, the purpose of the program to create unity and a positive attitude toward the school, to develop common ideals for the community and to develop leadership on the part of all.

The next step is for the community group to receive a newsletter indicating the benefit the students will receive through a public relations program. The total staff must be involved in the program. At the PTA meeting a brief presentation could be made; then various staff members could answer questions regarding the public relations program and the involvement of the school in the community. For additional support the community can be approached either in person or by telephone, or by letter stressing the focal points of the school and how the school is benefiting the children and the community.

Other means of reaching the community are usually overlooked. These are the vital positions of the custodians and the secretary in the school who see day to day operations, they see the influence and use of public relations and how the children benefit.

Other groups in the school can assist also. For example, the art class can make posters and displays for store windows, language arts classes can compose a newspaper that is mailed to all members of the community as well as writing letters to the editor of the newspaper and appearing on radio and television programs.

Science fair, band concerts, outdoor education, and various other segments of the school program can get involved in a public relations program.

Periodically a follow up study of students on the job and those attending a college or university should be utilized in promoting public relations programs. Results of performance on the job and in advanced classes at the university generally alleviate the fears of parents and they give better support to the school.

One of the most effective ways is systematically setting up a public relations program by developing a calendar. By simply listing the activities each month, the purpose of the activity and who is responsible for the activity gives the administration and faculty an overview of the total program.

For example, monthly newsletters could be mailed. Monthly radio series could be scheduled as well as television series. The school could use a slide presentation and a lecture series as well as a spot on the program at the PTA, at the orientation meeting during the first week of school. Information can be sent home with the grade reports as well as having various displays throughout the building during open house. Faculty can also plan an informal pot luck dinner or a coffee hour utilizing a simple form which simply says "I suggest..." This form gathers lots of good data both positive and negative which points out some of the ways a school can improve.

At all times the purpose of the public relations program must be to inform parents in the community of all the activities planned for each month and the issues relevant to the individual child's education. It also provides opportunities to listen to various guest speakers address parent groups and various school activities. We must continually utilize all types of media so the public is aware of the school and its impact on the community.

A simple check list of the school's public relations program could include:

1) The child is considered as an individual.

2) The public relations program is individualized for each child in the total district.

3) There is accurate reporting of the total cost and involvement of each teacher.

4) The public relations program is based on the curriculum and is not "window dressing".

5) The strength and weakness of each public relations topic must be reported and analyzed critically.

6) The administration, faculty, parents, and children must be involved in an in-service program in setting up the public relations program.

Individual contacts and personal relationships are the keys that are lasting and provide a sound working basis for parents and the community. A good public relations program will be a vital part of upgrading education in your district.

Philosophy of Education and the Curriculum

Why do we teach? What should we teach? How should we teach? These are questions that teachers must answer every day. When answering these questions teachers are expressing a particular philosophy of education and curriculum. These philosophies can be separated into two schools of thought, traditional and contemporary. The traditional philosophies include perennialism, idealism, and realism. Pragmatism and reconstructionism are considered more modern philosophies.

The traditional philosophies usually follow a more structured pattern than their counterparts.

In curriculum planning realist and idealist look for order and system. Traditionalists begin with what they feel a child should know. They provide the answers and the students learn by successfully reproducing someone elses answers. The perennialist concedes much of the precepts of idealism and realism, but differs largely, as do the realist and idealist, on which source to go to find the answers.

The pragmatist and reconstructionist place more faith in the abilities of children. They use curriculum to help children act responsibly, thoughtfully, and creatively. These philosophies feel that any curriculum can be interesting if it is organized at the child's level and fulfills his needs. Where the traditionalist provides the answers, the pragmatist and reconstructionist profess that no answer is ever final. They wish the learner to add his own thinking and to feel free to question, discuss, and create his own solutions. Both pragmatist and reconstructionist strongly agree that children must use an inquiry process and recognize the problem before seeking the answer; but they also disagree on several points. The greatest is that the reconstructionist looks to the future, he feels that the pragmatist, be devoting attention largely to the individual, ignores group interaction and the growth of the whole society.

While philosophy a teacher chooses to follow while teaching depends on numerous factors. The two most important factors are the needs of the students and the teacher's personal convictions. Some students may need drill and note work, others may be able to work independently to research their problems. If a teacher's personal feelings are too strong to be flexible, perhaps he or she should find a more suitable environment. Frequently administrators adapt a particular philosophy that they feel will work best for their school.

As a student teacher, you must be able to recognize the philosophy of your school. By observing teachers, becoming familiar with policy and procedure, and talking with faculty and staff you can become familiar with, and understand, the philosophy of the school. This is important if you expect to fully meet the needs of the pupils. Change sometimes moves very slowly and the philosophy of a school cannot be disrupted immediately by a student teacher. If the philosophy of the school is different than your own, try adjusting your thinking to fit that philosophy. As a future teacher you may find it necessary to change philosophies several times, depending on where you teach and what philosophy works best in a given situation.

Psychology of Learning

Two goals of education that have remained consistant, even through the changes in philosophy and procedures, are the transference of knowledge and intellectual development. The first goal places the responsibility of teaching a child about his world with the schools. The second states that the schools must help the child learn how to apply his knowledge to any situation.

How this learning process takes place is divided into two theories. The stimulus-response theory and the cognitive theory. Each theory believes itself to be totally exclusive and capable of defining the whole spectrum of the learning process.

The stimulus-response or behaviorist theory centers around the fixed and invariant aspects of the learning process. The behaviorist approaches learning through a variety of teaching techniques. The most popular or best known method is most easily described as conditioning. When a student is exposed to a new concept or situation the proper responses must be acquired and maintained. The behaviorist achieves this by providing a reinforcement each time the correct response is given. Through this reinforcement the learner is conditioned to give the desired response when faced with a specific situation.

The cognitive or humanistic theory approaches the variant and thinking aspects of learning. The Humanistic approaches learning through problem solving, creativity and observation. They feel that children can perform in a guided self-directed atmosphere in which they are working independently accept responsibility. One area that the humanist frequently uses to achieve this is the childs' own experiences. When faced with a new situation a child must draw on the knowledge he has acquired from his own direct experience, or those he has observed. This method enables the child to create a variety of responses and choose his best solution.

Historically, schools have heavily leaned toward the behaviorist theory rather than the humanistic approach. This is partially due to the influence of certain educators in past years on the teaching profession. The majority of schools in the United States are still operating successfully with this plan. However, the humanist approach has enjoyed increased popularity in recent years. Many educators have found that the cognitive approach works exceptionally well in the open classroom schools.

Which approach is used in the classroom is largely determined by the classroom teacher, administrators, and the educational objectives of the school.

The successful teacher needs to know both theories in order to determine which is most practical in a particular learning situation. In many situations teachers can draw something from each theory to help achieve their personal teaching objectives and the goals of the school.

Child Growth and Development

Whenever we try to understand growth, it is well to remember the epigenetic principle which is derived from the growth of organisms in utero. Somewhat generalized, this principle states that anything that grows has a ground plan, and that out of this ground plan the parts arise, each part having its time of special ascendancy, until all parts have arisen to form a functioning whole. In postnatal existence radical adjustments of perspective as lying relaxed, sitting firmly, and running fast must all be accomplished in their own good time. With them, the interpersonal perspective also changes rapidly and often radically, as is testified by the proximity in time of such opposites as "not letting mother out of sight" and "wanting to be independent." Thus different capacities use different opportunities to become full grown components of the ever-new configuration that is the growing personality.

Alfred Baldwin compares the theory of child growth and development to a patchwork quilt: each has its own insulated domain of study and though theories occasionally share a border, they rarely overlap one another. Freud concentrates on personality, Piaget on cognition, Gestalt theory on perception, and stimulus theory on learning. While each is concerned in its own way with the child and with development, the points of view they take on these issues are so different that it is difficult for them even to argue effectively.

In the light of this, points where the theories do converge seem note-worthy, and their mutual assertions seem all the more compelling, holding the promise that they may one day be the building blocks from which a unified theory will be constructed. One such point of convergence is in the impulsi-vity of the preschooler. Kagan observed that preschool children tend to respond rapidly and make more errors than do older children in problem-solving tasks, while Freud noted that infants and preschoolers tend to demand immedi-ate gratification of their impulses - which he ascribed to the predominance of the id in their personalities. Another convergence is between Freudian theory and social-learning theory on the importance for socialization (including development of a conscience and a sex role) of certain features in the early environment such as the emotional tone of the family and the methods of child-rearing employed.

Perhaps the clearest convergence between theories occur in their respec-tive treatments of intellectual development. Piaget outlines a progression from direct sensorimotor functioning to an increased skill in dealing with the world symbolically, first through loosely organized preconcepts and later in terms of coordinated conceptual systems. Vgotsky concurs in postulating that the child's first concepts are complexes that evolve with age into hierarchial classifications, while Werner's theory believes that intellectual development consists of the gradual differentiation of an initial stage of goability in keeping with the organic unity in Piaget's sensorimotor stage between knowing the world and acting upon it. The Kendler's theory of conceptual development parallels Piaget's in postulating the pre-dominance of a non-mediated

125

single-link stimulus-response made of processing in the two year old and the increasing use of a conceptually mediated mode as the child grows up.

The Psychological development that starts at birth and terminates in adulthood is comparable to organic growth. Just as the body evolves toward a relatively stable level characterized by the completion of the growth process and by organ maturity, so mental life can be conceived as evolving toward a final form of equilibrium represented by the adult mind.

Skills and Techniques of Teaching

Teaching techniques are the processes, manipulations, and procedures that teachers use to help children learn. Your student teaching experiences provide the opportunity for you to become familiar with the various techniques and helps you develop the skills to use them.

Teaching techniques vary with each teacher and school. A technique that works well for one teacher may not work at all for another. Every teacher should be familiar with as many different methods as possible, even if they have not mastered the skills to use them.

There are some basic techniques that the majority of teachers agree on. As a student teacher you will become most familiar with these.

Students usually have to be motivated before they begin a new lesson. If a lesson is presented in a stimulating, interesting way, students will be internally motivated. However, if this is not the case, then some incentive or prize must be introduced to externally motivate a pupil. If an incentive is needed, try to develop abstract prizes, such as honor rolls or special privileges. Many teachers have found that material incentives sometimes develop into the goal rather than as a means to the goal.

Learning activities can provide pupils with purposeful and productive experiences, while achieving specific teaching objectives and goals. Some of the more common methods are group or individual projects using concrete materials, plays or skits on a particular topic, students making graphs, charts, or pictures after researching information. Some other frequently used techniques include research papers, oral reports, and book reports.

A popular technique with many contemporary teachers is problem solving. Teachers provide the students with an open ended problem to solve. There are a few important characteristics of a good problem. It must deal with a practical problem. It should be stated clearly. It should be challenging, but be within the ability of the learner. It should be based on previous experiences of the pupil. Demonstrations are excellent ways to motivate and teach new concepts. It provides the students with the opportunity to learn through seeing and develops important observation skills which can be used later. If you are giving the demonstration, be sure you are properly prepared before beginning.

Two of the most common techniques are drill work and review. When using these methods, be sure not to over use them. Children can become bored very quickly if forced to do repetitious work continuously.

A fast growing technique is the classroom learning center. The learning center moves away from conventional teacher-textbook learning toward student experience learning. Learning centers can be used effectively in group work and individualized programs.

Question and answer method of teaching is one of the most effective techniques available for teachers. This technique also requires the most skill. The questions should be stimulating and of interest to the students.

These are just some of the teaching techniques available to teachers. While you progress as a teacher, you will become familiar with many more methods.

Teachers must also have methods of evaluating their techniques and pupil progress. The list of evaluating techniques is endless, but there are some well tested methods available. Observations, conferences, group discussions, and analyzing questions are excellent methods for checking pupil progress. Objective tests work well in most subject areas and can include a variety of elements such as completions, multiple choice, or matching questions. When evaluating, teachers should follow certain guidelines. The evaluation technique should be in pupil terms, realistic for the grade level, must be measurable and obtainable, to a degree, by all students. These guidelines can help make your evaluation effective and reliable.

Self-Renewing Teachers

There are not too many self-renewing teachers in the profession and therefore it behooves us to work exceptionally hard on factors of change and self-renewal. There must be motivation or a desire to change or an individual must be dissatisfied with himself or the status-quo in order to continue to grow and develop.

The profession requires certain skills and we must have this knowledge before we can change. There needs to be a drive or an effort for change by the teacher and the environment must allow for change.

One must remember that changes are not automatic and there is no such thing as one change. A change will continue to involve other changes and may also cause conflicts. The fewer people involved in change the more likely change will come about. That is, if there is to be change in the classroom it is much easier to change individual classrooms and not try to change the district overnight.

A teacher must have a set of priorities in order to implement change. They must be able to detect and determine where change is needed and how they can continue to grow and be self-renewing. We must remember that a basic model for change can be perfected and refined. The self-renewing teacher should set some type of goal each year and strive toward improving not only himself/herself but work for greater involvement of the students.

We must be able to build human resources and utilize all facets of the community in education. There are great resources in each community of individuals whether they be senior citizens or professional or non-white collar workers who have great things to contribute to the school.

The self-renewing teacher will build good interaction through love, trust, empathy, and loyalty. Though intangible, these are very important and are the very basis for growth and development.

We consider teachers as resources for children and children as resources for other children and for teachers. If we look into the community, we can immediately see the great resources of parents and volunteers that could be utilized in the educational process.

The teacher must choose wisely the goals and the best combination of resources to achieve the best type of learning for the students. We must realize that human resources are expandable and there is probably no end to what the self-renewing teacher can bring to the students in his/her classroom.

We have a great need for placing emphasis on student change and how it can be identified and what behavior maybe evaluated. At each step, the needs and the goals of the teachers are recognized and provisions are made for individualization through inservice training programs or additional graduate courses.

For self-renewal there must be some assumptions and foundations.

Through quality in-service institutes teachers may work with other staff members, parents, individuals in the community, or "expert" people to systematically bring about change. We must realize that change comes slowly, however, and I am sure we will readily realize that there are many committee and inservice days that are a complete waste of time. Self-renewing teachers must work exceptionally hard to bring about programs and actions in committees and through in-service days that will vitally affect the learning of the child. It is easy to say that the school system has the responsibility for providing teachers with both resources and tools to perform completely. However, as one visits schools, it is readily apparent that resources and tools vary greatly from one school to another even within the same districts, and that this is not a good criteria to evaluate the progress and success of the elementary teacher.

By attending quality institutes and functional committees, one is able to obtain vast resources of "inexpensive" materials that can be utilized in the classroom. Also much information is available in various community and professional offices.

We know that professional growth accrues from a variety of experiences. One has to identify the needs that are common among teachers and utilizing their experiences in education, we should be able to move more rapidly in upgrading the teaching profession.

The self-renewing teacher will take a lead and responsibility through staff development activities. He will help establish a plan to retrain teachers and to redirect activities into new channels of endeavor.

Most people readily recognize that there must be some incentive for continual growth and development. Provisions are usually made for salary increments and some feel a more productive way is through released time during the school day so that the teacher may continually work toward improving his or her efforts with and for children.

In today's society it takes a great commitment for teachers to continue to be self-renewing and not "die on the vine" while we see so many teachers both young and older who are there in the classroom just collecting their checks each month.

So we are saying that we need reforms in teacher education. We have always known that human beings have different personal qualities and have different background preparation. And it would be most alarming if all prospective teachers were standardized in their conceptions, aims and intellectual processes as well as in their understanding and the skills that they use in their individual classrooms.

So we must take some steps to change and improve the programs by the shifting of courses or adding of new materials. However, we must guard against the continual addition of new materials without reevaluation every three to five years of the total curriculum and our goals for each particular class.

We know that in planning programs to meet today's needs we must not find a single curriculum but we must systematically plan opportunities within each program for our students. The program must be flexible and offer a wide variety of resources so that there can be room for continuous change as needed within each field of knowledge and with each unique individual teacher and/or student.

Sometimes we have become so enamored with organizational and technological changes such as team teaching or modular scheduling that we fail to really look at the true purpose of teacher education. We tend to jump from one activity to another without really evaluating.

We seem to routinely do what we already know about the educational process, the nature of children and youth, the nature of subject matter, the nature of the educational setting, the nature of school and society, the nature of the process of learning, the nature of teaching, the nature of instructional methods and materials and media, the nature of one's individual self, the nature of the profession, the nature of evaluation, as well as other dimensions in teacher education without due consideration to new or improved information that would invite change in our old ways. As educators and self-renewing teachers we try through our acquisition of self-knowledge, experience and training to really determine what is appropriate for the education of children within our individual communities. We must also recognize that it is our job to foster learning and develop people who can learn and work together. So we must keep up with politics of change and the unexpected in the school.

We recognize that through education we have the single most powerful resource for eliminating racism and sexism, injustice and corruption and pollution and poverty. Yet we cannot seem to reach these goals as leaders in our individual communities. We must reach them in our individual communities if we cannot reach them from a state or national level first. We must continue to teach values of our community, state, and nation. We must recognize in our attempt for self-renewal and change in the system that even though we train the new teachers, they are soon to be swallowed up by the system. Most teachers now are between forty and fifty years old and have twenty to twenty-five years of teaching and are known as "career" teachers. We must reeducate them right along with the new teachers if we are to improve the goals of education significantly.

Not only must we bring outer change but we must bring inner change on the part of the teacher. For the career teacher, inservice workshops well planned and coordinated with follow up support are indispensible for educational change. We cannot just hold teachers "accountable" unless we give them an opportunity to learn new skills and understandings before we can expect them to improve. We must also recognize that we cannot retrain or reeducate those career people between 8:00 a.m. and 5:00 p.m. There must be some release time provided or an opportunity to attend a one or two week intensive inservice program.

We must move the university level into the classroom and work "hand and glove" with the teachers in the field to bring about the change. Too often we hear the graduate student saying this teacher does not know where it is at!

They have been so long at the university level and not in the field that they have not kept up with the change and therefore are not training teachers for the present day schools.

We must replace the present system with some type of partnership with teacher training institutions. By working in partnership we can better utilize both the financial resources and the personnel for each unique area that the university serves.

We need charismatic or magical leaders who are in positions of authority and power and see the importance for bringing about educational change. Much time can be spent discussing theory and philosophy. One does not need to "reinvent the wheel" but to deal with the practical realities of today's educational problems.

We must stress more learning through doing in our schools and society. We must restructure and eliminate "dead wood." We must have time to look at new materials and prepare materials that will bring about change. We must teach for transfer of training.

It is alarming for example that the State of Oregon has recently passed legislation mandating that all high school students have the skills to (1) complete the Oregon Income Tax Form (2) complete the Federal Income Tax Form and (3) be able to operate a car according to the state rules and regulations. It is disastrous to think that we as educators must "sit around" and wait for legislation action to bring about change. If the new math is or was not meeting the needs of individuals in the State of Oregon, then the teachers should have been the first to recognize that the students graduating from high school could not figure state or federal income tax.

We know that the methods used in the past indirectly affect the type of thinking used and the degree of creativity and intellectual development of students. So we must give them greater experience. We must provide an environment favorable for work with both intrinsic rewards and creative rewards. We must realize and recognize that there are so many practical things that we can use in our schools to approach and change learning. However, we must recognize that sometimes in extreme environments there can be hostility.

So we must build our own self concept where we have the security as teachers to accept, love, and work with all types of individuals and open their doors to the great international world.

Teacher Evaluation

In order to get a true picture of oneself and to recognize abilities and build on these as well as recognize areas of concern or weaknesses we must have evaluation. We know that our supervisors, co-workers, students and the community are holding teachers accountable for what goes on during the school day.

If you are not at the present time doing some type of self-evaluation, then you should begin immediately. One cannot look into the crystal ball or read tea leaves but evaluation is here to stay. The states of California, South Dakota, and Washington have mandated legislation for teacher evaluation. We find with the continual pressure on the public for additional taxes and more and more of the school budget (approximately eighty percent) now going for teachers' salaries there is strong pressure on principals and superintendents

135

to hire only outstanding teachers whether they have tenure or not.

Ratings can be formal or informal. They must have a framework based upon performance. Since we are being evaluated and judgments are being made for reemployment, transfer, and recognition of talents, or salary increases, we must provide some type of non-threatening environment so that we can evaluate ourself and have others evaluate us.

Instead of destructive gossip or working to avoid evaluation yourself, try putting yourself in other one's moccasins. Perhaps we might ask the question, "Why is the administration pushing self-evaluation?" or "Why are other teachers pushing self-evaluation?"

We know that evaluation brings about the improvement of the teacher and the improvement of instruction. These are the real goals of evaluation, so we must take time to think and evaluate.

In a non-threatening environment we must try to look at the areas of responsibility of the teacher, one's self - what is your job and what is your goal? We must ask ourselves "Are we really mature enough to do self-evaluation?" "Are we really able to look at ourselves and see how we are affecting the quality and quantity of learning of our products (children - future generations)." "Are they - the products - being turned out with rough workmanship - with flaws or can we do a better job?" In this throw-away generation are we throwing away our children's education?

If the public becomes the inspectors - like we have on assembly lines in various factories, then we can reject those teachers for not producing. And I am not saying schools are factories. But I am saying that we can learn a lot from the social and business world. The public (including some teachers) are beginning to demand results. They are beginning to demand better products for their money and everyone knows that money talks. So what are we as individuals going to do?

Teacher evaluation is troublesome, it is going to take time, it is going to take work, but there IS a workable solution. We must be practical and we can deal with problems of teachers and teaching and how to best help the teacher improve his or her instruction.

The current practices of evaluating teachers are shocking.

1. Evaluation is threatening to teachers.

2. They see it as something that is done to them by someone else.

3. It is used mostly for determining teacher status relative to dismissal, tenure and promotion, even though instructional improvement is often advertised as a major purpose.

4. Teachers often are unaware of the criteria used to judge them.

Now let us turn our attention to the way that teacher evaluation should be handled;

1. Evaluation should be something that the teachers anticipate and want because it gives an insight into their own performance. How does this compare with the threatening aspect to teachers?

2. It should be something in which teachers have a part along with students, parents, and administrators. How does this compare with it being something that is done to them by someone else.

3. Evaluation should be used to diagnose teacher performance so they can

strengthen their weaknesses through inservice education. How does that compare
- it is used to determine teacher status relative to teacher dismissal, tenure,
and promotion, even though instructional improvement is often advertised as
the major purpose.

4. Teachers should take part in developing or selecting evaluation instruments, so that they know the criteria by which they are judged. Compare that
with 4 - teachers are often unaware of the criteria used to judge them.

A National Education Association survey reveals that only about half of
the school systems follow any type of formal procedure in evaluating the teachers
and for the most part this present procedure is inadequate. Written ratings
are typical. Principals or superintendents are the ones responsible for these
evaluations.

Indirect methods of evaluation such as (1) Gathering impressions of the
teacher outside the classroom - noting his professional activities - gathering
impressions of him from students. (2) Appearance of the classroom such as
tops of desks, blinds are all even, etc. (3) Studying student's achievement
records. (4) Listening to what other teachers or parents say about him or her.

It is interesting to note that three or four principals or superintendents
expressed confidence in this evaluation. However, over fifty percent of the
teachers do not. They say it's unfair. Then how would you rate yourself?

Only about thirty four percent of the secondary teachers are observed,
usually about five minutes at a time and usually only once during the school
semester or year. Elementary teachers usually receive two visits during the
year.

Since 1966 there has been a strong trend in evaluation. This means the teacher should analyze his own performance and select aspects of his behavior for improvement. One of the major problems in education is to weed out unfit teachers. Rather, than attempt to prove at a hearing that a teacher is unsatisfactory the administration will merely ask or transfer them to another school or another district which simply SHIFTS THE PROBLEM AND DOES NOT SOLVE IT. But schools are beginning to be very selective for granting tenure. Some schools are building cases so they can dismiss teachers. The union or association in some cases is no longer protecting them. The teacher has to produce. The union must protect those qualified and weed out the unqualified in order to upgrade the profession.

In the meantime, many, many children and the public suffer. It is interesting to note that many administrators admit that the curricular changes, the new emphasis, special education and other rapid changes in the field of education, keep them from feeling that they have adequate background to evaluate. Then the teacher must evaluate himself or herself or arrange for a qualified individual to evaluate and discuss. This is especially important with over eighty percent of the district's money going for salaries. The taxpayers are demanding better schools so we have to have some type of systematic evaluation and improvement in learning. It is imperative.

A research study by Arthur Boyess reveals two classes of methods of rating teachers:

1. The general impression method - really not a method but a variety of approaches - teachers were rated - good or bad or indifferent - worthy or

unworthy of retention and promotion - all by the opinion of those who judge them. There is no teacher input.

2. The second approach was the analytical method - attempting to analyze particulars in teachers that might make them superior or inferior. Such things as discipline, instructional skills, scholarship, cooperation and loyalty, plans and methods, personality, professional interest, manner, poise, daily preparation, accuracy and promptness, attitude toward students, and appearance and health.

One of the biggest problems in rating is the area of "communications." Perhaps we should rate under five specific headings:

1. Personal Equipment - which is accuracy, tact, physical, mental, and moral qualities.

2. Social Equipment - which is involvement in the community, the profession, and most important working with children.

3. School Management - discipline, classroom management and the class routines.

4. Techniques of Teaching - including aims, skills, and stimulating thought, skills in questioning, skills in teaching, and techniques in how to study.

5. Results - shown by response of the class, student progress, general development, and moral influence.

If we are going to evaluate a teacher using external appraisal, we would observe the teacher's behavior. This is difficult because an outsider will have trouble evaluating the classroom situation and then communicating to the

140

teacher what improvement is needed. In other words, it all depends upon the eye of the beholder as to how and what the ratings are and how often the evaluator comes into the classroom and how many conferences they have with the individual teacher.

We may observe personality characteristics and patterns. However, we do not know what personality patterns lead to teaching success.

We can observe intelligence, we can look at college grades, we can observe knowledge of subject matter. However, research gives us only slight indications of the relationship between the intelligence, college grades and the knowledge of subject matter on one hand and the teacher's success on the other hand.

We can observe desirable changes in student behavior. The changes in student behavior can be observed. This message holds promise but there are problems. What are the effects and/or the influence of the media or outside interests such as clubs, television, influence of parents on student behavior.

We can observe the teaching process. This also appears to be promising. We can record selected aspects of the teaching such as teaching methods, teacher objectives, and teacher expression. We must set guidelines and measure according to these guidelines.

We can also do self-appraisal. If we do this there should be a helping role from the supervisor or another teacher. Changes can best occur in a non-threatening atmosphere. The participation of teachers in a program of self-appraisal must be <u>voluntary</u>. Freedom of choice to enter into the program must be absolutely guaranteed for each teacher. However, the administration and school board must set a time factor, for example three or five years, that all faculty members will take part in the evaluatory program.

Some assumptions of teacher evaluation are to consider the mental process which is more than thinking. Basically it involves human interaction where learning is the objective.

Teaching is not a single pattern of "most successful" behavior. Each teacher, therefore, must be free to devote his or her unique style to teaching.

Teacher behavior can be changed only by one person. That is, the teacher himself. No amount of commanding or extortion by the administration can actually change the teacher's behavior for the better. Teacher's behaviors are most readily changed when the teacher is provided objective data of his or her own teaching.

What are some of the actual steps of appraisal of oneself. How can we really rate ourselves? How can we really set forth a plan to evaluate today, tomorrow, or three months from now?

So let's start now. We can keep a record or mental note of how much we talk. How much do the students talk? When is there silence? What about our facial expressions? Are they frowning, neutral or smiling? What annoying mannerisms such as scratching one's head, etc.

It is very easy to begin self evaluation by simply getting an audio tape and turning it on. One can then hear the sounds, the tones, the interaction, and so on in the room. However, it is much better to be videotaped where one can see and hear what is going on in the room. I would strongly suggest that one look for specific things after you have been videotaped or audiotaped. The teacher should keep the tape the first time and if they feel comfortable, can then ask the principal, or the department head, or "an old pro" to sit in and evaluate.

In three weeks one can then look at the performance on the job and get an idea if they are satisfactory or above average or outstanding. One can look more objectively at the preparation for class and how the class responds. One can evaluate the time plan, the organization plan, and perhaps even make a time and motion chart.

Then by the end of three months, one should be able to really do some good self-evaluation using student evaluation forms or administrative evaluation forms or perhaps peer evaluation forms. One can evaluate the teacher's role during the day as far as clerical tasks, using automatic devices, the interaction of children and so forth.

Some other ways for evaluation might be using student achievement by talking with present or past students (this depends on the grade level) and particularly surveying the high school graduate three or five or ten years after graduation. Some schools use objective and structured tests to check student achievement.

Committees can be elected or selected by the faculty to evaluate other peers. This evaluation must be in a variety of situations and be repeated many times. Let me stress that after any type of evaluation of a teacher by another individual or group there should be immediate feedback through a conference to share positive and constructive ideas toward improvement. The teacher should never be left dangling. They need to know about their job performance. Are they going to get tenure, promotion, a good salary increase or are they not going to be retained.

Schools use the relationship of the school and community as part of their evaluation and teachers are judged by their service to the community. There are many cases where teachers have been suspended or fired because of beards, their appearance (i.e. no ties, T shirts, cut offs and so forth), their marital life, or their consumption of alcohol or drugs and so forth.

Sometimes evaluation includes teachers growth through professional activities such as college courses, educational travel, committee work or publication of articles or books.

It is most important that each district work out a composite plan that is non-threatening to the teachers and that fits that specific community.

Some other things to consider in evaluation are the individuals' rating of performance which would include background preparation and whether or not the individual is teaching their major or minor area. Also to be considered is the improvement of self through proper frame of mind and attitude for growth and development.

In evaluation we must be able to recognize, identify and correct weaknesses from among a number of different alternatives. We must be able to translate, to transfer, and to give information into new words and/or phrases. We must be able to infer, to derive needs, to arrive at new conclusions. We must look beyond the surface. We must create. We must make use of thought and imagination.

There are many types of available forms for evaluation. However, before we look at the different areas of concern of the various evaluative forms we should consider whether we are a product oriented teacher or a process oriented

144

teacher.

If you are a product oriented teacher you use very little or no use is made of diagnostic measures to assess students interests, strengths, and needs. The teacher makes all or most of the assignments for the students. The teacher's talk is mostly yelling, lecturing, asking cognitive-memory, or convergent types of questions and correcting and evaluating students' work or behavior. Most of the students are working on teacher-made assignments or projects in such content areas as language arts, math, social studies, and science. The teacher checks papers and gives grades. The teacher sets up a time schedule as to when to bring closure to lessons, chapters, units, and so forth. The teacher tries to adhere to an established routine. Children are taught to wait for appropriate times to present their ideas, interests, and needs.

If you are a process oriented teacher then you diagnose and assist students in their interest, their strengths and their needs. The teachers are guiding and helping the student make choices in relation to his/her own interests, strengths, and needs. Students eventually make their own decisions. The teacher's talk is mostly questioning, asking in the area of critical thinking, accepting, praising, supporting, and encouraging children. Most students will be directing their own learning in relation to the goals they have chosen from a variety of options. (Options could be set by students when they are ready and until that time, they are set by the teacher.)

Teachers are guiding and encouraging the students to check their work. Evaluations will be a joint venture with the teacher and student and then lead to self-evaluation. Students must have some or total say in making the decision as to when they're finished with a topic or unit. Teachers exhibit spontaneity, flexibility, and openness in making provision for and responding to students ideas, interests and needs.

One should look carefully for the thread that weaves throughout all the evaluation forms. One must stress again that any type of evaluation should be tailor-made for the individual district.

Developing Self-Concepts

One of the major emphasis in teaching children is to help them develop a better understanding of themselves, a better self-image or self-concept. Many teachers get very concerned about "learning" and do not recognize nor realize what a vital part a positive self concept plays toward bringing peace, harmony, and understanding to the individual.

Love is probably the one word that would give us the best basis from which to build toward developing a positive self-concept. Children nurtured in a loving environment by parents and teachers both at home and in school are more likely to develop a good self-concept, a feeling of worthiness and a positive outlook leading to successful experiences. Love provides a happy motivation toward continued growth and self development. So, it seems that our first concern should be for each individual teacher to have a good self-concept, to view himself clearly, closely and accurately and to be at peace with one's self he will in turn have an improved outlook toward and a relationship with children.

If we tried to define self-concepts, if we tried to apply it to ourselves before we begin working with others then how do we really see ourselves? How should we see ourselves and how should our love reflect? Gaze for a moment into a mirror and see how you see yourselves. How do others see you? Can we place ourselves in the other one's mocassins? There is an old Indian saying that to understand another individual's point of view we should be able to place ourselves in their mocassins and view the situation or problem through their eyes.

Let us try to define self-concept. It is learned by each person through his lifetime of experiences with himself, with other people and the realities of the external world. It is a frame of reference to which the individual interacts with his world. The self-concept is powerful, it is meaningful, and it is complex. It must be stable and it must be consistent. It is inter-action, it's a frame of reference through which the individual interacts with himself and the world.

Research gives us two indications of the self-concept. One of these concepts is children who hold themselves in low esteem tend to be backward or under-achievers. Whereas the children with positive self-concepts tend to learn well and to relate to others. We must expect children to build positive self-concepts. Success or failure is learned early in life and it is related directly to one's self. Self-concepts can be related to one's drives. Self evaluation has a profound effect on one's thinking. Self con-cepts involve emotions, desires, values, and goals. How does a person deal with these emotions, with these desires, with these values, and with these goals? Does he evade them? Does he repress them? Does he distort them? Does he have a feeling of personal growth and strength?

If we are to develop a good positive self-concept, somehow we must build in the traits of honesty, responsibility, loyalty, moral courage, and friend-liness. We must be able to have these elements in a fairly stable and fairly consistent world. We must provide those basics for the children to learn the values all by themselves.

We find values are not automatic. Self-concepts are not automatic. They're not gifts and they are not things we can give our children or things they inherit. The values have to be learned by valuing, by growing through prizing, through cherishing, through appreciation, through esteeming and through holding dear. Knowing and doing are two different things. We must be doers, we must be knowers and we must be realists. If we are doers then we must get involved with people. If we are knowers we use our knowledge to help people and in this world we must be very realistic.

So it takes special talents, intelligence, and social ability. These are the real things that influence children. We must set examples as parents, teachers and people in the community by rewarding those young children when they do positive things.

Nothing is as damaging to children as examples set by parents or teachers when they say "do as I say and not as I do." We find the daily things experi-enced by children are those that are most important to him and the patterns that are set as children can be directly related to their adult life.

Children today can not be children - they are young adults. So we must work together to develop a good positive self-concept. It is quite difficult when we are working with parents from broken homes or homes where there is very low income.

What type of individual are you? Are you a self-directed individual? Are you submissive? Are you defiant? Are you maladjusted? Or are you mixed? The self-directed individual is one who sets high standards for himself. He seldom is satisfied with his performance, he's abmitious, he works, he's persistent, he's conscientious, he's orderly. Such a person is one who is responsible, one who is honest, one who has leadership qualities, one who accepts leadership responsibility, (even though he doesn't always enjoy it), one who knows the difference between right and wrong, one who lets children learn to accept themselves and their abilities whether they're above average or below average. We see the self-directed individual as one with less emotional warmth than the average person, so security results from performance. If they really perform, they are secure. Achievement is important, particularly in childhood. He feels the worth not for himself but for his accomplishments. There is a strong sense of self.

The adaptive individual is one who has this type of self concept. He's one who is sociable, friendly, vivacious, outgoing, he's good in social environments, he enjoys leadership but doesn't strive hard to get it. His attributes are that he tends to be a conformist, he's generally above average in intelligence, he usually has good health, he has good sex appeal, he's usually permissive, he's tolerant, he has a strong sense of himself and he's non-aggressive.

The submissive individual is one who will not take action, he waits for others to take the lead, he is non-aggressive, he does not want to be in

149

authority, in fact he lives by authority, he's physically unattractive, he likes emotional warmth. He conforms to standards, therefore, he has security. He has a weak sense of self or not a good self-concept.

A defiant individual is one who is hostile to society, he does poorly in school. He refuses to conform to society, he attacks property, he is destructive, he breaks the laws, he bears grudges, he has difficulty in holding jobs, he never sacrifices for others, he has a poor development or a poor sense of self.

The maladjusted, of course, are the individuals who are discontented, they're insecure, they're frustrated with their homes, their families or their work. However, they are not openly hostile or they do not do things against society or individuals. They try to relate to the environment. They try to live up to certain standards, they want to become self-directed, or adaptive or submissive, but they're caught, and consequently they can not move in one direction or another direction. They're individuals who have mixed self-concept and about a third of the people fit in this particular class. These are the individuals that have traits of two or more of those discussed.

After one evaluates carefully himself and applies the criteria to individuals in his classroom he can make a simple list of what he wants that child to experience daily. What kind of patterns does he want the child to relate to? What kind of child do you want him to turn out to be? We need to know where we are going otherwise we might end up somewhere else. It seems to me that in developing a self concept we must be accountable to know where we are going. We have to know what goals we are trying to attain, and if we do not we are liable to wind up somewhere else. We're likely to have total confusion and the child will have frustrations and inabilities to deal with problems in society.

We must individualize a program for each child and/or the family as we can not just at random say this is going to work or that is going to work. I think we need to set down some concrete things working with the individual and/ or small groups because you cannot impose your self-concept upon people.

You have to make a list of positive things by which to improve self concept and then formulate a plan to implement these. Perhaps the real key is the ability and willingness to plan and to put this plan into practice; to be convinced that the plan is good, that it is a sound plan and to stick to that plan. We need to continue to evaluate and reevaluate. The plan has to have imagination and the individual must be willing to take the time to go through the things they need. We must give praise and we must have adequate time for the child. One of the easiest things to do to kill self-concept development is simply to say these are the things I am going to do, these are the things I am going to measure and impose them upon the individual.

I'm trying to say that we have to have realistic goals and the things can be achieved. Individuals can feel success and this success can be measured. We have to be willing to change plans and goals and we have to be willing to accept a few failures. But we must keep track of the progress and these are the things we need to report on and to avoid the negative aspects. In goal planning and development for self-concepts don't shoot for the moon. Look how many years and hundreds of years and centuries it has taken man to go from the time of Adam and Eve till the time the first man walked on the moon.

We need to know what resources we have and what manpower as well as finances are needed to achieve the goals that we have worked out together. We need to be able to really communicate and to hear and understand.

One of the main ingredients in developing good positive self-concepts is "a heavy dose of common sense." It's easy sometimes to say this is the way, this is how it should be done, but when children are concerned about the next meal or about shoes when the weather is zero then they're not going to be concerned about self-concept. If the parents are concerned over many of the social, emotional or economic situations that push from all sides then they are not going to be concerned about the individual's self-concept, they are going to be more concerned about "survival."

We must have a simple designed way to accomplish things. There is a great difference between making a beautiful sand candle with a little bit of sand and wax and a wick and some are just as beautiful as the highly molded candles. So lets first make sand candles, simple candles before we make the highly molded candles. We must remember that we can not mold children because children have both good and bad qualities. We must work with the good qualities to overcome the bad qualities, we must have simple goals and express them in terms that people can understand. We must be practical and we must remember that they cannot be evolutional nor revolutional. We must plan to go slowly at first. We must plan the program over a long period of time. We know that we cannot have an over-complex or over-ambitious program.

We first must crawl, then walk and then run. But, let's not crawl for years and years. Let's set our goals of crawl, walk and then run. Remember we must be accountable while realizing that it is very hard for human beings to change because we are all products of our heredity, our education, our environment, and our experiences.

There's not much we can do about our heredity. We might be able to do something about future generations as far as the population explosion is concerned, but education is one of the real keys. The environment and the experiences that children receive within these environments are things we must be greatly concerned with. So remember there is an educational environment, there is a socioeconomic environment, there is a cultural environment, there is a home, family, and religious environment. These are all interacting. These are the real keys we have in education and they must go hand in hand.

What can we do to promote parents and teachers to work with children to develop a better self-concept? Let me list some things for you to consider.

For developing positive self-concepts; specific recommendations -

1. Help students to develop pride in their work and a feeling of self worth.

2. Try to understand the changes that take place in the world.

3. Learn how to respect and to get along with people with whom we work and live.

4. Learn how to respect and to get along with people who think, dress, and act differently.

5. Develop good character and self-respect.

6. Learn how to be a good citizen.

7. Understand and practice democratic ideas and ideals.

8. Develop skills in reading, writing, speaking, and listening.

9. Learn how to examine and use information.

10. Prepare students to enter the world of work.

11. Practice and understand the ideas of health and safety.

12. Understand and practice the skills of family living.

13. Learn how to be a good manager of time, money, and property.

14. Learn how to use leisure time.

15. Help students appreciate culture, and beauty in their world.

16. Develop a desire for learning now and in the future.

We must be patient, understanding, listen and hear and let love radiate in order to help individuals develop a good positive self-concept.

OTHER TITLES AVAILABLE FROM
CENTURY TWENTY ONE PUBLISHING

NEW DIRECTIONS IN ETHNIC STUDIES: MINORITIES IN AMERICA by David
    Claerbaut, Editor   Perfect Bound   LC# 80-69327
    ISBN 0-86548-025-7 $9.95
COLLECTING, CULTURING, AND CARING FOR LIVING MATERIALS: GUIDE FOR
    TEACHER, STUDENT AND HOBBYIST by William E. Claflin   Perfect
    Bound   LC# 80-69329   ISBN 0-86548-026-5 $8.50
TEACHING ABOUT THE OTHER AMERICANS: MINORITIES IN UNITED STATES
    HISTORY by Ann Curry   Perfect Bound   LC# 80-69120
    ISBN 0-86548-028-1 $8.95
MULTICULTURAL TRANSACTIONS: A WORKBOOK FOCUSING ON COMMUNICATION
    BETWEEN GROUPS by James S. DeLo and William A. Green   Perfect
    Bound   LC# 80-69328   ISBN 0-86548-030-3 $11.50
LEARNING TO TEACH by Richard B. Dierenfield   Perfect Bound
    LC# 80-69119   ISBN 0-86548-031-1 $10.95
LEARNING TO THINK--TO LEARN by M. Ann Dirkes   Perfect Bound
    LC# 80-65613   ISBN 0-86548-032-X $11.50
PLAY IN PRESCHOOL MAINSTREAMED AND HANDICAPPED SETTINGS by Anne Cairns
    Federlein   Perfect Bound   LC# 80-65612   ISBN 0-86548-035-4
    $10.50
THE NATURE OF LEADERSHIP FOR HISPANICS AND OTHER MINORITIES by
    Ernest Yutze Flores   Perfect Bound   LC# 80-69239
    ISBN 0-86548-036-2 $10.95
THE MINI-GUIDE TO LEADERSHIP by Ernest Yutze Flores   Perfect Bound
    LC# 80-83627   ISBN 0-86548-037-0 $5.50
THOUGHTS, TROUBLES AND THINGS ABOUT READING FROM THE CRADLE THROUGH
    GRADE THREE by Carolyn T. Gracenin   Perfect Bound
    LC# 80-65611   ISBN 0-86548-038-9 $14.95
BETWEEN TWO CULTURES: THE VIETNAMESE IN AMERICA by Alan B. Henkin and
    Liem Thanh Nguyen   Perfect Bound   LC# 80-69333
    ISBN 0-86548-039-7 $7.95
PERSONALITY CHARACTERISTICS AND DISCIPLINARY ATTITUDES OF CHILD-
    ABUSING MOTHERS by Alan L. Evans   Perfect Bound   LC# 80-69240
    ISBN 0-86548-033-8 $11.95
PARENTAL EXPECTATIONS AND ATTITUDES ABOUT CHILDREARING IN HIGH RISK
    VS. LOW RISK CHILD ABUSING FAMILIES by Gary C. Rosenblatt
    Perfect Bound   LC# 79-93294   ISBN 0-86548-020-6 $10.00
CHILD ABUSE AS VIEWED BY SUBURBAN ELEMENTARY SCHOOL TEACHERS by David
    A. Pelcovitz   Perfect Bound   LC# 79-93295   ISBN 0-86548-019-2
    $10.00
PHYSICAL CHILD ABUSE: AN EXPANDED ANALYSIS by James R. Seaberg
    Perfect Bound   LC# 79-93293   ISBN 0-86548-021-4 $10.00
THE DISPOSITION OF REPORTED CHILD ABUSE by Marc F. Maden   Perfect
    Bound   LC# 79-93296   ISBN 0-86548-016-8 $10.00
EDUCATIONAL AND PSYCHOLOGICAL PROBLEMS OF ABUSED CHILDREN by James
    Christiansen   Perfect Bound   LC# 79-93303   ISBN 0-86548-003-6
    $10.00
DEPENDENCY, FRUSTRATION TOLERANCE, AND IMPULSE CONTROL IN CHILD ABUSERS
    by Don Kertzman   Perfect Bound   LC# 79-93297   ISBN 86548-015-X
    $10.00
SUCCESSFUL STUDENT TEACHING: A HANDBOOK FOR ELEMENTARY AND SECONDARY
    STUDENT TEACHERS by Fillmer Hevener, Jr.   Perfect Bound
    LC# 80-69332   ISBN 0-86548-040-0 $8.95
BLACK COMMUNICATION IN WHITE SOCIETY by Roy Cogdell and Sybil Wilson
    Perfect Bound   LC# 79-93302   ISBN 0-86548-004-4 $13.00

SCHOOL VANDALISM: CAUSE AND CURE by Robert Bruce Williams and Joseph
    L. Venturini   Perfect Bound   LC# 80-69230   ISBN 0-86548-060-5
    $9.50
LEADERS, LEADING, AND LEADERSHIP by Harold W. Boles   Perfect Bound
    LC# 80-65616   ISBN 0-86548-023-0 $14.95
LEGAL OUTLOOK: A MESSAGE TO COLLEGE AND UNIVERSITY PEOPLE by Ulysses
    V. Spiva   Perfect Bound   LC# 80-69232   ISBN 0-86548-057-5
    $9.95
THE NAKED CHILD THE LONG RANGE EFFECTS OF FAMILY AND SOCIAL NUDITY
    by Dennis Craig Smith   Perfect Bound   LC# 80-69234
    ISBN 0-86548-056-7 $7.95
SIGNIFICANT INFLUENCE PEOPLE: A SIP OF DISCIPLINE AND ENCOURAGEMENT
    by Joseph C. Rotter, Johnnie McFadden and Gary D. Kannenberg
    Perfect Bound   LC# 80-69233   ISBN 0-86548-055-9 $8.95
LET'S HAVE FUN WITH ENGLISH by Ruth Rackmill   Perfect Bound
    LC# 80-68407   ISBN 0-86548-061-3 $6.95
CHILDREN'S PERCEPTIONS OF ELDERLY PERSONS by Lillian A. Phenice
    Perfect Bound   LC# 80-65604   ISBN 0-86548-054-0 $10.50
URBAN EDUCATION: AN ANNOTATED BIBLIOGRAPHY by Arnold G. Parks
    Perfect Bound   LC# 80-69234   ISBN 0-86548-053-2 $9.50
DYNAMICS OF CLASSROOM STRUCTURE by Charles J. Nier   Perfect Bound
    LC# 80-69330   ISBN 0-86548-052-4 $11.50
SOCIOLOGY IN BONDAGE: AN INTRODUCTION TO GRADUATE STUDY by Harold A.
    Nelson   Perfect Bound   LC# 80-65605   ISBN 0-86548-051-6 $9.95
BEYOND THE OPEN CLASSROOM: TOWARD INFORMAL EDUCATION by Lorraine L.
    Morgan, Vivien C. Richman and Ann Baldwin Taylor   Perfect Bound
    LC# 80-69235   ISBN 0-86548-050-8 $9.50
INTRODUCTORY SOCIOLOGY: LECTURES, READINGS AND EXERCISES by Gordon D.
    Morgan   Perfect Bound   LC# 80-65606   ISBN 0-86548-049-4
    $10.50
THE STUDENT TEACHER ON THE FIRING LINE by D. Eugene Meyer   Perfect
    Bound   LC# 80-69236   ISBN 0-86548-048-6 $11.95
VALUES ORIENTATION IN SCHOOL by Johnnie McFadden and Joseph C. Rotter
    Perfect Bound   LC# 80-69238   ISBN 0-86548-045-1 $4.50
MOVEMENT THEMES: TOPICS FOR EARLY CHILDHOOD LEARNING THROUGH CREATIVE
    MOVEMENT by Barbara Stewart Jones   Perfect Bound   LC# 80-65608
    ISBN 0-86548-042-7 $8.50
FROM BIRTH TO TWELVE: HOW TO BE A SUCCESSFUL PARENT TO INFANTS AND
    CHILDREN by Gary D. Kannenberg   Perfect Bound   LC# 80-69331
    ISBN 0-86548-043-5 $7.95

DATE DUE

MAR 1 9 1980			
MAR 2 0 1989			
GAYLORD			PRINTED IN U.S.A